OSPREY AVIATION ELITE • 6

Jagdgeschwader 54
'Grünherz'

SERIES EDITOR: TONY HOLMES

OSPREY AVIATION ELITE • 6

Jagdgeschwader 54 'Grünherz'

John Weal

OSPREY
PUBLISHING

Front cover
One of the brightest stars in JG 54's firmament during the early months of the campaign against the Soviet Union was Leutnant, later Oberleutnant, Max-Hellmuth Ostermann. This ex-*Zerstörer* pilot had been credited with just nine kills prior to the launch of *Barbarossa*. However, against the Red Air Force he revealed his natural ability as an outstanding dogfighter. His score began to escalate rapidly as the 'Green Hearts' supported the German Army's advance towards Leningrad. Jim Laurier's specially-commissioned cover painting captures an incident that took place during the first winter of the war in the east. Ostermann, the *Staffelkapitän* of 7./JG 54 in his 'White 2', was engaged on a *'Freie Jagd'* sweep with his wingman when they came to the aid of a group of Ju 87s from StG 2 'Immelmann'. The dive-bombers had done their work well, as witness the columns of smoke rising from the enemy target on the far side of the lake. But now the returning Stukas found themselves under attack by Polikarpov I-153 fighters. These agile biplanes were a common adversary of the 'Green Hearts' during the opening stages of Barbarossa, and many were included among the final tally of 93 Soviet aircraft which Ostermann claimed destroyed before he was himself killed in action on 9 August 1942

First published in Great Britain in 2001 by Osprey Publishing
Midland House, West Way, Botley, Oxford, OX2 0PH, UK
443 Park A Avenue South, New York, NY 10016, USA
E-mail: info@ospreypublishing.com

ISBN 978 1 84176 286 9

CIP Data for this publication is available from the British Library
Edited by Tony Holmes
Page design by Mark Holt
Cover Artwork by Jim Laurier
Aircraft Profiles and Badge Artwork by John Weal
Map by John Weal
Origination by Grasmere Digital Imaging, Leeds, UK
Printed and bound in China through Bookbuilders
Typeset in Adobe Garamond and Univers

08 09 10 11 12   11 10 9 8 7 6 5 4 3 2

ACKNOWLEDGEMENTS
The Author would like to thank the following individuals for their generous help in providing information and photographs.

In England – Chris Goss, Michael Payne, Dr Alfred Price, Jerry Scutts, Robert Simpson and W J A 'Tony' Wood.

In Finland – Kari Stenman.

In Germany – Herren Manfred Griehl, Norbert Hannig, Walter Matthiesen and Holger Nauroth.

EDITOR'S NOTE
To make this new series as authoritative as possible, the Editor would be interested in hearing from any individual who may have relevant photographs, documentation or first-hand experiences relating to the world's elite units, their aircraft Force, and the crews that flew them, in the various theatres of war. Any material used will be credited to its original source. Please write to Tony Holmes at 10 Prospect Road, Sevenoaks, Kent, TN13 3UA, Great Britain, or by e-mail at: tony.holmes@zen.co.uk

For details of all Osprey Publishing titles please contact us at:

NORTH AMERICA
Osprey Direct, C/o Random House Distribution Centre, 400 Hahn Road, Westminster, MD 21157
E-mail: info@ospreydirect.com

ALL OTHER REGIONS
Osprey Direct, The Book Service Ltd, Distribution Centre, Colchester Road, Frating Green, Colchester, Essex, CO7 7DW
E-mail: customerservice@ospreypublishing.com

Or visit our website: **www.ospreypublishing.com**

CONTENTS

THE PARTS OF THE SUM

*J*agdgeschwader 54 – the famous 'Green Hearts', one of the most successful Luftwaffe fighter units to operate on the eastern front – was very much a product of the war years. Unlike other, more senior *Jagdgeschwader*, which had enjoyed the benefits of peacetime activation and working-up, the 'Green Hearts' *Geschwader* did not even exist as such when hostilities broke out on 1 September 1939.

It was not until July 1940, and the eve of the Battle of Britain, that three hitherto separate and disparate *Jagdgruppen* would be amalgamated to add a completely new *Jagdgeschwader* – bearing the number 54 – to the Luftwaffe's order of battle.

The oldest of these three *Gruppen* stemmed directly from the Austrian air arm of 1938. When Germany annexed her south-eastern neighbour on 12 March of that year, Austria's modest *Luftstreitkräfte* included two fighter formations. Although termed *Jagdgeschwader*, these were the equivalent of a Luftwaffe *Jagdgruppe* of the period, and comprised just three *Staffeln* apiece.

JaGeschw I (1., 2. and 3. *Staffeln*) at Graz-Thalerhof had been operating a mix of Fiat CR.20bis and CR.30 biplanes for some while. Activated more recently, *JaGeschw* II (4., 5. and 6. *Staffeln*) at Wien(Vienna)-Aspern was equipped with Fiat CR.32bis fighters. It was the latter which was selected to provide the nucleus for a new Luftwaffe *Jagdgruppe*.

And little time was lost in assimilating the bulk of Austria's military strength into the German *Wehrmacht* (armed forces). The German army was to be the major beneficiary to the tune of some half-dozen divisions. But for the Luftwaffe the major prize was undoubtedly *Jagdgeschwader* II. At 1030 hrs on the morning of 12 March 1938 the first of some 30 Ju 52 transports had landed at Wien-Aspern. They were followed almost

Italian Fiat **CR.32bis fighters of the pre-war Austrian *Luftstreitkräfte's* JaGeschw II. The men and machines of this unit would form the nucleus of what was to evolve into the *Jagdgeschwader* 54 *'Grünherz'***

German and Austrian officers of I./JG 138 at Wien-Aspern. They are, from left to right, Oberleutnant Brustellin (*StaKa* 1), Leutnants Gärtner and Ewald, Oberleutnants Maculan (*StaKa* 2) and Mader (*StaKa* 3) and *Gruppenkommandeur* Hauptmann von Müller-Rienzburg

immediately by the Do 17 bombers of II./KG 155. A *Staffel* of Bf 109B fighters (3./JG 135) arrived soon thereafter.

On 28 March, at a ceremony held on the airfield of Wiener Neustadt (Vienna New Town) some 40 miles (64 km) to the south of the Austrian capital, *Generalfeldmarschall* Göring himself presented Oberleutnant Wilfried von Müller-Rienzburg, the *Kommandant* of *Jagdgeschwader* II, with a new unit standard. Four days later, on 1 April, von Müller-Rienzburg's command was formally incorporated into the Luftwaffe as I./JG 138.

Two of the new *Jagdgruppe's* component *Staffeln* were straightforward redesignations from the now defunct Austrian unit, 2. and 3./JG 138 having previously been 4. and 6./*JaGeschw* II. They were commanded by Oberleutnants Alois Maculan and Anton Mader respectively. Maculan had been a member of Austria's first 'covert' military flying training course of 1930-31, and Mader had attended the second such course in 1931-32.

Five of the six graduates from the class of 1930-31 – including Alois Maculan – would be killed on active service during World War 2. Only Anton Mader would survive the war, having risen in the interim to the position of *Kommodore* of JG 54.

By contrast, the now Hauptmann von Müller-Rienzburg's one-time 5./*JaGeschw* II, commanded by Leutnant Erich Gerlitz (class of 1930-31), had departed Austrian soil to become the new 3./JG 135 at Bad Aibling in neighbouring Bavaria. And, in exchange, the vacant 1./JG 138 slot was to be filled by redesignating the original Bf 109B-equipped 3./JG 135 – the Luftwaffe *Staffel* which had flown in to Wien-Aspern on the first day of the *Anschluß*. Under its new guise 1./JG 138 was commanded, as before, by Oberleutnant Hans-Heinrich Brustellin.

During the course of the war that was to come, the attrition among the pilots, and the resultant influx of fresh replacements, meant that – in the air, at least – the 'Austrian' character of the *Gruppe* would inevitably be

At first the *Gruppe's* Fiat CR.32s retained their silver finish and Austrian serials, with only the national insignia being overpainted to indicate change of ownership. Later, at least some of these machines would be given a coat of Luftwaffe camouflage (see colour profile 1). The aircraft closest to the camera appears to one of the handful of two-seat CR.32s supplied to Austria

diluted. But the ground personnel would remain predominantly Austrian throughout the next seven years.

For a brief period 2. and 3./JG 138 retained their silver Fiat biplanes. At first, the inverted white triangle and red-white-red rudder striping of the Austrian air arm were simply replaced by the Luftwaffe's *Balkenkreuz* and swastika. Later, the Italian machines were given a coat of camouflage paint, and it was at this juncture that the *Gruppe* badge first appeared. The 'Lion of Aspern', commemorating Napoleon's defeat outside Vienna in 1809, was chosen in honour of the unit's home base.

Although 1./JG 138 continued to operate their Bf 109s, at least one source suggests that they, too, had some Fiats on strength. The *Gruppe* also received a handful of ex-JG 135 Heinkel He 51 biplanes for training purposes. Organisational changes at higher levels resulted in the Wien-Aspern *Gruppe* becoming I./JG 134 on 1 November 1938, by which time the entire unit had standardised on Bf 109Cs and Ds.

Another change of identity was to take place on 1 May 1939. This was the date which saw the introduction of the greatly simplified 'block' system of unit designation (whereby all *Geschwader* within *Luftflotte* 1 were numbered in block 1-25, those within *Luftflotte* 2 in block 26-50, and so on). As the first *Jagdgruppe* operating under the control of *Luftflotte* 4 in the south-eastern area of the Greater German Reich, von Müller-Rienzburg's *Gruppe* was consequently renumbered I./JG 76. At the same time the unit's Bf 109Cs and Ds began to give way to the newer E variant.

The wholesale redesignations of 1 May 1939 also resulted in the first fleeting appearance of a 'JG 54' in Luftwaffe records. Ten months earlier,

In May 1939 I./JG 76 took delivery of its first Bf 109Es. Like 1. *Staffel's* 'White 9' (Wk-Nr 6009) in the foreground, all the aircraft seen here are wearing the Vienna *Gruppe's* 'Lion of Aspern' badge introduced the previous year

on 1 July 1938, a second *Jagdgruppe* had been activated at Bad Aibling alongside I./JG 135, the Bavarian unit which had participated in the annexation of Austria.

Initially known as II./JG 135, by November 1938 this *Gruppe* had moved to Herzogenaurach, north-west of Nürnberg, where it became I./JG 333. Upon the introduction of the block system its number then changed to I./JG 54, which proclaimed it to be the first *Gruppe* of the fourth *Jagdgeschwader* operating under the control of *Luftflotte* 3. It retained this position, and designation, for exactly a fortnight, for on 15 May 1939 it was transferred to Fürstenwalde and there inducted into the recently established *Zerstörer* arm as II./ZG 1.

By this time – the early summer of 1939 – the spectre of all-out war was looming large in Europe. The Luftwaffe's carefully structured, but still as yet incomplete, long-term expansion programmes of the preceding years went by the board as the pace of mobilisation was hastily stepped up. In June 1939 the High Command ordered the activation of five completely new 'emergency' *Jagdgeschwader* to begin the following month.

In the event, none of the five ever reached full establishment. But a number of *Jagdgruppen*, or partial *Jagdgruppen*, were created as a result of this last-minute crash programme.

One such was formed around a cadre of personnel provided by I./JG 1, the only *Jagdgruppe* then stationed in the Reich's isolated north-eastern-most province of East Prussia. I./JG 1 was just completing re-equipment with the Bf 109E, and was therefore also in a position to provide the fledgling formation with a full complement of its cast-off Bf 109Ds.

Commanded by Hauptmann Martin Mettig, the new *Gruppe* was officially activated on 15 July 1939 as I./JG 21. Mettig's three *Staffelkapitäne* were Oberleutnants Günther Scholz, Leo Eggers and Georg Schneider. For the first few days of its existence, I./JG 21 shared I./JG 1's base at Jesau, some 15 miles (25 km) south south-east of Königsberg, before then moving closer to the provincial capital by taking up residence at Gutenfeld, only five miles (8 km) from the outskirts of the city, on 24 July.

I./JG 21 acknowledged the part I./JG 1 had played in its creation by choosing a similar unit badge to that worn by its 'parent' unit – the German Crusader's cross, the coat-of-arms of Jesau, with the silhouettes of three Bf 109s superimposed – albeit in different colours. And just like I./JG 76 in the far south with its unmistakable Austrian 'feel', so I./JG 21's ground staff would reflect its Prussian origins throughout its subsequent six-year history.

Situated between the two geographical extremes of East Prussia and Austria (or the 'Ostmark' – the 'Eastern Marches' – as the former independent state of Austria was officially known after its annexation into the Greater German Reich), Herzogenaurach in central Germany had already housed the first, short-lived I./JG 54 just two months

Pictured at Gutenfeld in August 1939, armourers work on the 7.9 mm MG 17 fuselage machine guns of a Bf 109D of I./JG 21. Although the *Gruppe* badge – the 'Crusaders' Cross of Jesau – is all but invisible in the reflected glare of the sun below the windscreen, the three yellow rings on the spinner identify this *Dora* as a machine of 3. *Staffel*

earlier. Now, in mid-July 1939, it was chosen as the site for another of the 'emergency' *Jagdgeschwader* hastily set up during the last few weeks of uneasy peace in Europe.

'*Jagdgeschwader*' was to prove something of a misnomer, however, for the new unit – JG 70 – did not manage to attain even *Gruppe* strength. It comprised no more than two *Staffeln*: 1./JG 70, commanded by Oberleutnant Reinhard Seiler, and 2./JG 70, led by the grandly named Hauptmann Hans-Jürgen von Cramon-Taubadel. Nevertheless

it, too, would be imbued with its own regional character, for most of the ground personnel had been recruited from Upper Franconia.

Such, then, was the position and status of I./JG 21, I./JG 70 and I./JG 76 as the war clouds gathered. Three *Gruppen* – only one of which could measure its previous history in terms of months, the other two having been in existence for less than seven weeks – widely dispersed across the face of the Reich, originating from different regions and backgrounds, and none bearing any discernible relationship or affinity with another.

THE CAMPAIGN IN POLAND

Launched at first light on the morning of 1 September 1939, the invasion of Poland involved two of these three *Gruppen*.

On the northern flank the 37 serviceable Bf 109Ds of Hauptmann Mettig's I./JG 21 (together with I./JG 1's Bf 109Es) formed the sole single-engined fighter component of *Luftwaffenkommando Ostpreussen*. This command, which controlled all Luftwaffe units based in the province of East Prussia, was cut off from the rest of the Reich by the intervening Polish corridor.

Leutnant Joachim Schypek (right) poses in front of 3./JG 76's 'Yellow 13' – the numeral usually worn by a *Staffel's* reserve aircraft – at Wien-Aspern in the last piping days of peace. Schypek's war would last just over a year before being brought to a halt following a belly-landing in Kent towards the close of the Battle of Britain

On 17 August 1939 – exactly a fortnight prior to the outbreak of hostilities – I./JG 76 moved from Wien-Aspern to Stubendorf, in Upper Silesia. The stacked rifles, helmets and personal kit indicate that transfer is not yet complete. But however long it takes, one airman is not going to go hungry – note the large loaf centre foreground!

The principal task of *Lw.Kdo.Ostpreussen* in the coming conflict, however, was not to assist in the occupation of the corridor, and thereby establish a link-up with the main body (that was the responsibility of forces striking eastwards out of Pomerania), but rather to support the East Prussia-based 3. *Armee* as it advanced due south on Warsaw.

In keeping with the then current doctrine, both I./JG 21 and I./JG 1 officially came under the direct control of regional air-defence HQ at Königsberg.

The original intention behind the 1938 splitting of the Luftwaffe fighter arm into 'light' single-engined Bf 109 fighter units and 'heavy' twin-engined fighter (i.e. Bf 110 *Zerstörer*) units was that the former were to be retained on home soil primarily for aerial defence duties, leaving the latter to undertake the more offensive roles campaigning 'in the field' alongside the *Kampf-* and *Stukagruppen*.

This meticulous division of labour – a perfect example of peacetime pedantry – did not last a day in practice. Within hours of the first shots being fired, I./JG 21 was transferred from Gutenfeld down to Arys-Rostken, a small forward landing strip in the south-east of the province close to the border with Poland.

From this rolling, tree-girt meadow (it did not get much more 'in the field' than Arys-Rostken!) Mettig's pilots took off on their first offensive mission of the war in the mid-afternoon of 1 September. Their orders were to escort *Lw.Kdo.Ostpreussen's* bombers and Stukas in a second wave of attacks on Polish airfields in the Warsaw area. Whether it was due to their relative inexperience operating as a unit, or unfamiliarity with the task they had been called upon to undertake, is uncertain, but things did not run smoothly.

Fighters of the Polish Pursuit Brigade rose to intercept the attackers, and elements of I./JG 21 became embroiled in a scrappy series of engagements lasting well over 30 minutes. By the end of that time they had accounted for four of the enemy (a fifth claim remained unconfirmed). The first to score was 3. *Staffel's* Leutnant Fritz Gutezeit, whose opponent went down near the Polish capital at 1655 hrs.

As one Bf 109D of I./JG 21 trundles in overhead, another gets the once-over from its groundcrew. The mechanic peering up at the starboard mainwheel leg attachment point, and the bent tip of just one propeller blade, would seem to indicate a problem – perhaps a minor taxying accident, or a nose-over on Arys-Rostken's less than even surface

Safely arrived at Stubendorf, pilots and groundcrew of I./JG 76 await events as the tension mounts. According to one source, this group in front of Olt Franz Eckerle's 'Yellow 1' are listening to the daily news bulletin, a suggestion borne out by their rapt expressions

A second Pole fell to future *Experte* and Oak Leaves recipient Leutnant Gustav Rödel of 2./JG 21 in the same area nearly a quarter of an hour later. A third was credited to Oberleutnant Georg Schneider, *Staffelkapitän* of 3./JG 21, shortly thereafter and the fourth to one of Schneider's NCO pilots, Unteroffizier Heinz Dettner. The last two Poles had both been shot down north of Warsaw as the raiders retired.

All four of the above pilots apparently claimed their victims as 'PZL P.24s'. But the enemy fighters were, in fact, almost certainly PZL P.11s, as this was the type which equipped the squadrons of the Pursuit Brigade based at Warsaw-Okecie. The P.24 was a development of the earlier machine, intended solely for the export market.

A belated Polish order for 70 P.24s was cancelled immediately prior to the outbreak of war, and it is believed that only one P.24 – a pre-production model – was operated by the Polish air force during the conflict.

The *Gruppe* paid a high price for its four confirmed kills, however. Six of its Bf 109s failed to return, with five pilots being forced to land behind enemy lines, mainly from lack of fuel. They were all captured. The sixth put his aircraft down in neutral Lithuania. Fortunately, all six later returned safely. Seven other machines suffered varying degrees of damage, and at least two more became lost and landed away from base.

Gruppenkommandeur Hauptmann Martin Mettig, meanwhile, had been wounded in the hand and thigh early in the melee when a flare cartridge exploded in his cockpit as he tried to fire off a recognition signal in a vain attempt to dissuade a group of over-eager Heinkel He 111 gunners from shooting at his fighters! Altogether, it was not an auspicious baptism of fire.

I./JG 21 was given little time to lick its wounds. Although the initial objective of this first *Blitzkrieg* campaign in the history of warfare – the neutralisation of the enemy's air power – was quickly achieved, and encounters with the Polish air force became a rarity after the first week of fighting, the *Gruppe* was not kept idle. Lacking opposition in the air, it was increasingly committed to ground-strafing missions against the Polish army divisions retiring southwards towards Warsaw.

After its hard-won aerial victories on the opening day, the *Gruppe* achieved just two further kills. On 6 September Oberleutnant Leo Eggers, the *Staffelkapitän* of 2./JG 21, despatched a 'P.24' close to the Polish capital. Twenty-four hours later, fellow *Staffelkapitän* Oberleutnant Georg Schneider claimed the *Gruppe's* sixth and final victim of the campaign – and his second – by shooting down yet another of the enemy's high-winged fighters some 45 miles (72 km) north north-west of Warsaw.

On this same 7 September 2. *Staffel's* Leutnant Gustav Rödel was forced down during a ground-strafing sortie. It is not clear whether this was as a result of combat damage or mechanical failure. But, luckily, Rödel had already made it back almost as far as the border. He managed to avoid detection and returned to the *Gruppe* the following day.

A number of Bf 109s were damaged by light anti-aircraft and small-arms fire during the course of the low-level attacks which occupied the remainder of I./JG 21's time in Poland. But the only two fatalities resulted from a mid-air collision between two 3. *Staffel* machines near Gehlenburg on the East Prussian side of the frontier.

Towards the end of September the *Gruppe* was recalled from its forward position at Arys-Rostken and ordered back to Jesau. With a reported total of no fewer than 19 of its fighters destroyed or written off, Hauptmann Mettig's I./JG 21 had suffered by far the highest casualty rate of all the nine Bf 109-equipped *Gruppen* actively engaged against the Poles. The unit had single-handedly contributed close on 30 per cent of the overall total of 67 Bf 109s lost during the campaign.

By comparison, I./JG 76 in the south – which, coincidentally, would also claim six victories plus one unconfirmed – escaped relatively lightly. Before hostilities commenced, the ex-Austrian *Gruppe* had undergone several changes. Two of von Müller-Rienzburg's *Staffelkapitäne* had been posted to other units, 1./JG 76 now being commanded by Oberleutnant Dietrich Hrabak and 3./JG 76 by gifted aerobatic pilot Oberleutnant Franz Eckerle. Both would rise high in the ranks of the later JG 54, and be awarded the Oak Leaves in the process.

In mid-August 1939 I./JG 76 had left Wien-Aspern for Stubendorf, in Upper Silesia. From here it was transferred to a forward landing ground near Ottmuth, close to the German-Polish frontier. This was to be the *Gruppe's* jumping-off point for the forthcoming attack on Poland. For unlike I./JG 21, which remained within the borders of East Prussia throughout its part in the campaign, I./JG 76 was scheduled to move up into occupied territory to keep pace with the advancing ground forces.

Their unit's assigned tasks were twofold. First it would escort the massed Stukas of Generalmajor von Richthofen's *FliegerFührer z.b.V.*, based at Ottmuth and surrounding fields, as they attacked Polish air force targets in the Cracow area to the south-east. Once this threat to the ground-troops' right flank had been eliminated, the Bf 109 pilots – and the Stukas – were tasked with supporting the armoured spearheads of 10. *Armee* as they drove north-eastwards towards Warsaw.

Foggy conditions on the opening day impeded the pre-emptive strikes against the enemy's air bases.

The tranquility of this scene belies the fact that a state of war now exists, not just with Poland, but against the western Allies too. For close examination of the original print reveals a single white victory bar on the tailfin of 3./JG 76's 'Yellow 9' in the middle distance. This is almost certainly the aircraft of Uffz Willi Lohrer, and dates the picture as post-3 September 1939, the day Britain and France declared war on Germany. In fact, further scrutiny shows the underwing cross to have been overpainted in preparation for the application of a larger size, full-chord cross of the kind carried as an added precaution by many of the Bf 109s engaged in ground-attack operations during the latter stages of the Polish campaign. Finally, note the parasol-winged He 46 of 4.(H)/31 (background right), one of only two *Staffeln* still flying this antiquated tactical reconnaissance machine in Poland

13

Nevertheless, the ground offensive was launched as planned. Within 48 hours – on 3 September, the day Britain and France declared war on Germany – the leading Panzers were across the River Warthe and advancing on Kamien to the south of Lodz.

While the Luftwaffe's Stukas were systematically blasting apart the improvised defences that the Poles were hastily preparing to protect the next natural river barrier, forward units of the German army were coming under attack from PZL P.23 Karas light bombers of the Polish air force.

The oversized wing crosses were meant to guard against 'friendly' flak at low altitude. But 2. *Staffel's* 'Red 1' has obviously caught a packet from someone. This is believed to be Feldwebel Leopold Wyhlidal ruefully surveying the damage which brought him down for the third time over Poland, north-west of Radom on 17 September

A pair of these rather slow, but rugged machines provided I./JG 76 with its first two victories on the afternoon of 3 September. The successful claimants were Leutnant Rudolf Ziegler of the *Gruppenstab* and 3. *Staffel's* Unteroffizier Willi Lohrer. Future *Experte* Oberleutnant Dietrich Hrabak, *Staffelkapitän* of 1./JG 76, also clashed with P.23s on this date, albeit with markedly less success. He forced-landed behind enemy lines, but was able to evade capture and return to his unit 24 hours later.

On 4 September Hauptmann von Müller-Rienzburg also claimed a P.23 light bomber in the Lodz region. Although the *Gruppenkommandeur's* kill was not confirmed, two 1. *Staffel* pilots had more luck the following day in the same area south of Lodz. Leutnant Hans Philipp (who was destined to become the *Jagdwaffe's* twelfth-highest scorer of the war, despite his relatively early death in action in 1943) and Feldwebel Karl Hier were each credited with a 'PZL P.24' (presumably P.11) fighter.

Despite heroic efforts on the part of the Poles, the German offensive was unstoppable. On 7 September I./JG 76 was transferred forward from Ottmuth to Witkowice, in Poland, in the wake of the advancing ground units. It was on this day that Oberfeldwebel Johann Klein claimed the *Gruppe's* fifth kill with the destruction of a P.23 Karas. Less than 24 hours later the leading Panzers were at the gates of the Polish capital.

As I./JG 21 had found on the northern front, Polish opposition in the air also began to decline along the southern sector after the first week's fighting. On 10 September the aptly named Leutnant Roloff von Aspern was responsible for I./JG 76's final victory of the campaign – yet another of the seemingly ubiquitous PZL P.23 light bombers. The next day, in one of the *Gruppe's* final encounters with the Polish air force, a 2. *Staffel* machine was damaged in a dogfight with an enemy fighter.

On this same 11 September the *Gruppe* made its second move in the space of five days. This time its destination was Kamien, which had been one of 10. *Armee's* initial objectives, and the scene of fierce fighting less than a week earlier. Although Polish air activity was in terminal decline, the enemy's anti-aircraft defences still posed a formidable threat – especially during low-level missions of the kind that I./JG 76 was now being ordered to carry out.

The *Gruppe* had lost a second Bf 109 over enemy territory on 9 September when Feldwebel Leopold Wyhlidal of 2./JG 76 forced-landed close to Warsaw after being hit by flak. Wyhlidal made his way back to Witkowice the next day, only to be brought down twice more during the course of the following week!

Several other machines were damaged by ground fire during this final phase of I./JG 76's Polish campaign. By the end of the second week, however, the *Gruppe's* tasks were essentially completed, and the first elements began to retire from Poland, first to Stubendorf, and thence back to Wien-Aspern. Before September was out the entire unit was once more enjoying the comforts of its home base on the outskirts of Vienna.

THE 'PHONEY WAR'

While I./JG 21 and I./JG 76 were in action over Poland, the two *Staffeln* of I./JG 70 had remained at Herzogenaurach. Here, subordinated to *Luftgaukommando XIII*, the local air command headquartered at Nürnberg some 12 miles (20 km) away, they were held at readiness to perform the role originally envisaged for the Bf 109 – homeland defence.

It was to prove an unnecessary precaution. Throughout the opening weeks of the 'Phoney War' Allied air incursions were restricted almost entirely to the Reich's immediate border regions – her frontier with France in the west, and along her North Sea coastal belt (both sides studiously sought to avoid violating the neutral Dutch and Belgian airspace which lay between these two 'fronts'). In fact, Nürnberg was not to be subjected to aerial bombardment until early in January 1940 – and then by nothing more lethal than a million or more propaganda leaflets!

In the interim, I./JG 70 had undergone fundamental changes. Plans for the establishment of a *Gruppenstab*, to be headed by Major Kithil, had been implemented before the outbreak of hostilities. Now Kithil's command was to be brought up to proper *Gruppe* status by the addition of a third *Staffel*.

Currently based alongside the Bf 109Ds of 1. and 2./JG 70 at Herzogenaurach were a clutch of more unusual machines. When Germany marched into what remained of Czechoslovakia in March 1939 (after Hitler's occupation of the Sudetenland the previous autumn, and Slovakia's declaration of 'independence'), she had automatically come into possession of a considerable amount of military hardware.

I./JG 70 was brought up to full establishment with the activation of a 3. *Staffel*, **equipped with ex-Czech Air Force Avia B 534s. Like I./JG 76's earlier Fiats, these 'foreign' biplanes did not last long, and were soon replaced by Bf 109s**

Among the booty were many of the Avia B 534 fighters of the ex-Czechoslovak Air Force. Like the Fiats of Austria's *JaGeschw* II before them, the Avia biplanes were quickly repainted in Luftwaffe markings. Courses were duly set up to familiarise German pilots and ground-crews with these machines. And it was the Avia *Lehrgang* at Herzogenaurach which was used to form a brand new 3./JG 70.

In the event, neither the Avias nor the above designation were to last long. The Czech biplanes soon gave way to Bf 109s, and on 15 September 1939 the entire *Gruppe* was redesignated to become a second I./JG 54. At the same time Major Kithil relinquished command to Major Hans-Jürgen von Cramon-Taubadel, erstwhile *Kapitän* of 2. *Staffel*.

Like the first, short-lived I./JG 54 back in May, the new *Gruppe* did not stay at Herzogenaurach for more than a few weeks. But its links with Franconia would be retained, as evidenced by the decision to adopt the coat-of-arms of Nürnberg – the regional capital – as the *Gruppe* badge.

I./JG 54's first destination upon leaving Herzogenaurach was Böblingen, some nine miles (15 km) to the south-west of Stuttgart. With the outcome of the campaign in Poland now a foregone conclusion, the Luftwaffe High Command was intent upon building up its fighter strength along the *Westwall* to guard against attack from the French. I./JG 54 formed part of the force defending the southern sector of the Reich's frontier with France, from Karlsruhe down to the Swiss border.

In the ensuing months of the 'Phoney War' the *Gruppe* would transfer temporarily to one of the southernmost fields of all, Friedrichshafen, on the shores of Lake Constance, where the machines were housed in the cavernous airship shed of the Zeppelin works. Later I./JG 54 would also be based briefly at Eutingen bei Horb, before finally making the short 17-mile (28 km) hop back to Böblingen.

The two *Gruppen* which had seen action over Poland were also slotted into the growing defences lining Germany's western borders. On 9 October the now Major Mettig's I./JG 21 flew in from East Prussia to Plantlünne. Twelve days later it moved to nearby Hopsten.

Although these two airfields were situated to the west of Osnabrück, and were thus opposite neutral Dutch, rather than French, territory, it was here that the first victory in the west was scored. On 30 October future *Experte* Leutnant Heinz Lange of 1./JG 21 caught a French-based RAF Blenheim (of No 18 Sqn) carrying out a reconnaissance of the area, and he shot it down some 25 miles (40 km) north-west of Hopsten.

The dangers inherent in operating close to a neutral frontier were brought home to the *Gruppe* the following month when, on 30 November, Leutnant Rexin lost his bearings whilst on a routine patrol and strayed over the Dutch border south of Venlo. Presumably short of fuel, he attempted to land on an invitingly straight stretch of road but was killed when his aircraft hit a building.

By this time I./JG 76 had also been transferred to the western front. Departing Wien-Aspern, and after a short stop-over at Gelnhausen, it arrived at Frankfurt Rhein-Main civil airport on 2 November. Here, too, the unit was able to enjoy all the comforts of an indoor dispersal by taking up residence in another of Germany's huge pre-war Zeppelin sheds.

Fortunately, this sybaritic existence did not impair its operational efficiency. Four days after I./JG 76's arrival in Frankfurt, Oberfeldwebel Max Stotz (who had joined the Austrian *Luftstreitkräfte* back in 1935, and who would subsequently rise to become one of the *Grünherz Geschwader's* highest scorers) brought down another reconnaissance Blenheim. Stotz's victim, a No 57 Sqn machine sent to probe the secrets of the *Westwall* defences, crashed near Bad Kreuznach, south-west of Mainz.

These early successes in the west were, however, to be somewhat offset by the events of 22 November. On that date two of I./JG 54's machines

One of two casualties from a clash between I./JG 76 and French Morane fighters over the Saarland region on 22 November 1939, the wreckage of Leutnant Heinz Schultz's 'Yellow 11' was later put on public display in the Champs Elysées in Paris. Note that what may appear to be a dark splinter camouflage on the rear fuselage is the shadow thrown by the tarpaulined tail unit

crash-landed out of fuel west of Eutingen. More seriously, two other Bf 109s of I./JG 76 came down behind enemy lines after clashing with French Morane MS.406 fighters.

Leutnant Heinz Schultz just failed to make it back across the border. He belly-landed into a field in the middle of the Maginot Line defences south of Saarbrücken and was quickly taken prisoner by French colonial troops. His damaged aircraft was later put on display in Paris, where it helped to raise money for a French Air Force charity.

The other casualty of the engagement with the Moranes over the Saarland frontier landed intact some 37 miles (60 km) away to the north of Strasbourg. NCO pilot Feldwebel Karl Hier was also captured. His undamaged mount, 'White 14', served a more practical purpose than that of fund raiser for the *Armée de l'Air*. It was thoroughly test flown by both the French and British, before finally being shipped to the USA in May 1942.

The three *Gruppen* remained on their assigned sectors of the western front – I./JG 21 to the north, I./JG 76 in the centre, and I./JG 54 in the south – throughout the remainder of the 'Phoney War'. For each of them it was a period (weather permitting) of mainly uneventful frontier patrolling, interspersed by occasional brushes with the enemy.

One such incident took place on 21 December when elements of I./JG 54, led by *Gruppenkommandeur* Major Hans-Jürgen von Cramon-Taubadel, attacked a French reconnaissance Potez and its dozen-strong escort of MS.406s over the east bank of the Rhine. After an untidy 50-mile (80 km) chase from Bühl down to Freiburg, honours were even. Major von Cramon-Taubadel was credited with one of the escorting Moranes.

The other victim of the 22 November engagement was landed intact by Feldwebel Karl Hier. His 'White 14' was subsequently test flown by both the French and British. It is seen here in *Armée de l'Air* colours, with the blue of the rudder tricolour foremost and the French roundel on the fuselage obscuring the second digit of the aircraft's original *Staffel* number

But Hauptmann Paulisch, *Staffelkapitän* of 2./JG 54, suffered leg wounds in the action and was forced to bail out of his damaged machine.

An easing of the wintry conditions during the second week of the New Year led to another sudden flurry of activity. On 10 January I./JG 54 again intercepted a reconnaissance Potez – this time unescorted – to the south of Freiburg. The intruder managed to escape back across the Rhine before being caught and brought down by Oberleutnant Reinhard Seiler, *Staffelkapitän* of 1./JG 54.

For 'Seppl' Seiler, who was already a nine-victory veteran of the *Legion Condor*, this was the opening shot of a wartime career with JG 54 which would see him add exactly 100 kills to the nine scored in Spain – a feat that would be duly recognised by the award of the Oak Leaves.

Unfortunately, during the low-level chase, one of Seiler's pilots was killed when Leutnant Schütz's aircraft struck the ground. A second accidental death occurred on the central sector on the same date. Leutnant Claus von Bohlen und Halbach of I./JG 76 was carrying out a routine high-altitude patrol over the Trier region when his Bf 109 was seen to plunge vertically into the ground, probably as a result of oxygen failure.

Forty-eight hours later, on 12 January, yet a third recce Blenheim (of No 114 Sqn) was claimed, this time north of Saarbrücken by I./JG 76's Leutnant Bernhard Malischewski. But although damaged, the British twin managed, in fact, to limp back into France before forced-landing. Unteroffizier Ernst Wagner of 2./JG 54 also came down on French soil – far less willingly, it must be assumed – when he had to take to his parachute after being attacked by an MS.406 west of the Upper Rhine on 19 January.

Meanwhile, on the northern sector, I./JG 21 had been transferred, via Krefeld and Münster, to München-Gladbach. It was here that Major Martin Mettig took his leave, passing command of the *Gruppe* to Hauptmann Fritz Ultsch. Mettig had been ordered to establish a *Geschwaderstab* JG 54, alongside I./JG 54 at Böblingen, and was appointed its first *Kommodore* with effect from 1 February 1940.

Further spells of adverse weather continued to hamper aerial activity over the western front in the weeks ahead, but as conditions slowly improved, the border sparring between the opposing fighter forces resumed. On 7 April a dozen Moranes 'bounced' elements of I./JG 54 west of Strasbourg, and Leutnant Paul Stolte was shot down by an MS.406 and captured. But another of the attackers provided Reinhard 'Seppl' Seiler with his second kill of the war.

A second clash with Moranes further to the south, over the Belfort region, 12 days later resulted in what is believed to be JG 54's first combat fatality when Leutnant Helmut Hoch's Messerschmitt exploded in mid-air.

Two days later still, on the afternoon of 21 April, the central sector witnessed one of the first recorded encounters between I./JG 76 and RAF fighters when a sprawling dogfight developed along the Luxembourg frontier. One of the Luftwaffe casualties was 2./JG 76's Feldwebel Leopold Wyhidal, who had possibly fallen victim to the No 73 Sqn Hurricane I of RAF ace Flg Off N 'Fanny' Orton. It was Wyhidal who had forced-landed on no fewer than three occasions during the brief campaign in Poland. But this time he would not return.

BLITZKRIEG IN THE WEST

The three *Gruppen* were to remain in their allotted sectors of the western front for the launch of *'Fall Gelb'* ('Case Yellow'), the invasion of France and the Low Countries scheduled for 10 May 1940.

In the north, still at München-Gladbach, Hauptmann Ultsch's I./JG 21 came under *Luftflotte* 2 control. It would operate as part of JG 27, the *Geschwaderstab* to which it had been subordinated (together with I./JG 1)

Oberleutnant Reinhard Seiler (left), *Staffelkapitän* of 1./JG 76, offers a light to his 3. *Staffel* counterpart, Oberleutnant Hans Schmoller-Haldy, during a cigarette break at a snowy Böblingen at the height of the 'Phoney War' in January 1940

since arriving at Plantlünne from East Prussia back in October. The units' task was to support the air and ground forces' initial assault on Belgian and Dutch frontier defences.

The central and southern *Gruppen,* I./JG 76 and I./JG 54, both formed part of *Luftflotte* 3, the 'air fleet' responsible for providing aerial cover for the main armoured thrust out of the Ardennes and the Panzers' subsequent drive across France to the Channel coast.

Commanded since February by Major Richard Kraut, I./JG 76 had moved up from Rhein-Main to Ober-Olm, on the left bank of the Rhine, on 17 April. It, too, remained subordinated to the *Geschwaderstab* – in this case JG 2 – under which the unit had operated throughout its period of 'Phoney War' service at Frankfurt.

I./JG 54 also had a new *Gruppenkommandeur*. When Hans-Jürgen von Cramon-Taubadel was appointed *Kommodore* of JG 53 on 1 January, his place at the head of I./JG 54 had been taken by Hauptmann Hubertus von Bonin, another *Legion Condor* veteran (with four kills) and latterly *Staffelkapitän* of 5./JG 26. Von Bonin's I./JG 54 was the only *Gruppe* of the three to enjoy the advantage of serving under its own parent *Geschwaderstab*, JG 54, with which it still shared Böblingen. And to bolster the *Geschwader's* numbers for the forthcoming assault on France, the same field also housed the temporarily attached II./JG 51.

The *Blitzkrieg* in the west began, as planned, before first light on the morning of 10 May 1940 with co-ordinated airborne strikes against Belgian and Dutch frontier fortifications along the northern flank. Operating under JG 27, the pilots of I./JG 21 were initially ordered to secure and maintain control of the airspace west of Maastricht. These first sorties of the day went virtually unopposed and resulted in only one kill, with *Gruppenkommandeur* Hauptmann Ultsch reportedly claiming the destruction of a Belgian Fairey 'Firefly' (but which was, in all probability, a Fox).

A second mission mid-morning saw the *Gruppe* escorting a formation of Junkers (some sources refer to Ju 87 dive-bombers, others to Ju 52s engaged in supply-dropping) north-west of Liège. This did result in a confrontation with the Belgian Air Force, which lost three of its Gloster Gladiator fighters to I./JG 21 – one each being credited to Oberleutnant Schneider, Leutnant Hans-Ekkehard Bob and Feldwebel Erwin Leykauf.

References also differ regarding the claims made by the *Gruppe* later in the day in the Tirlemont area, quoting either two further Gladiators brought down, or three aircraft – type unspecified – destroyed on the ground.

The second day of the campaign, which cost 1. *Staffel* a Bf 109 shot down by RAF Hurricanes (possibly of No 17 Sqn) over Rotterdam, ended with elements of the *Gruppe* moving forward to Peer, a small field some 11 miles (18 km) inside Belgium.

The unexpectedness of the opening airborne assault, and the speed of the German advance since, had taken the Allies completely by surprise. Air activity on 11 and 12 May was still concentrated mainly back along the frontier waterways – the River Maas (Meuse) and the Albert Canal – as Allied bombers sought belatedly to destroy the bridges over which German forces were now pouring in their thousands. But Hauptmann Ultsch's I./JG 21 continued to support the forward spearheads of 6. *Armee* in their diversionary drive towards Brussels.

On 12 May the *Gruppe* was credited with four Hurricanes destroyed (including a second victory for Oberleutnant Schneider) south-east of the Belgian capital. A fifth enemy fighter, identified as a French Bloch 152, was despatched near Namur. Twenty-four hours later three more RAF Hurricanes were claimed during dogfights over the Dyle Line (the main defensive position guarding the approaches to Brussels).

But towards the close of that same 13 May I./JG 21 moved to a forward landing strip in southern Belgium, where it lost one of its number to a French Curtiss Hawk 75. The 'feint' along the northern flank had served its purpose. The focal point of *'Fall Gelb'* was about to change dramatically.

As the French and British divisions vacated their prepared positions in north-east France and rushed forward to Belgium's assistance, they left in their wake a dangerously widening gap between themselves and the main body of the French army. Allied forces believed (as they were meant to!) that the airborne landings in Holland and Belgium presaged a repeat of the tactics which Germany had employed at the start of World War 1 – a powerful northern 'right hook' through the then, as now, neutral Low Countries.

In fact, the *Blitzkrieg* of 1940 turned the Schlieffen plan of 1914 on its head. The bulk of the *Wehrmacht's* armoured might had been massed in secret further to the south, along the wooded valleys and steep, leafy byways of the Eifel (the continuation of the Ardennes range into Germany). And it was the gap opening invitingly in the front of this force which was to be the major axis of the advance to the Channel coast.

While attention was turned to events in the north, the Panzers of 12. *Armee* emerged from their hiding places, brushed aside the thin screen of defenders guarding the 'impenetrable' Ardennes sector of the front, and charged headlong for the one barrier which stood between them and the open tank country beyond – the River Meuse.

In just over 72 hours, leading elements of 2. *Panzerdivision* were crossing the Meuse a few miles downstream from Sedan. Suddenly aware of the enormity of the danger which threatened if the invaders breached this river line in force, the French ordered every available bomber to concentrate on the Sedan bridgeheads, and requested that the RAF do the same.

Throughout the following day wave after wave of bombers, French and British alike, attacked the Meuse crossing points. But the Luftwaffe was equally determined to protect the strategically vital bridges. The *Jagdgruppen* were waiting in numbers – by the day's end over 800 individual sorties had been flown – and they exacted a devastating toll. As night fell *Jafü* 3 calculated that close on 90 Allied aircraft had been shot down in the vicinity of Sedan. The war diary of II. *Fliegerkorps* christened 14 May 'The Day of the Fighters'.

Although I./JG 76 was not among the highest scoring of the units involved, it did play a significant part in the day's many actions. The *Gruppe* had been oredered forward from Ober-Olm to Wengerohr on 11 May. From this small strip above the Moselle Valley, Oberstleutnant Kraut's Bf 109 had begun patrolling

During the opening stages of the campaign against France an unknown pilot of Schmoller-Haldy's 3./JG 76 belly-landed this 'Yellow 3' near Sedan. A bored soldier of the Signal Corps sits guard on the cowling, his helmet balanced on the cockpit roof, awaiting the arrival of the recovery team

the Sedan-Charleville stretch of the Meuse two days later. On 14 May itself each pilot flew at least three sorties or more.

At around midday one *Staffel* clashed with 15 French Curtiss Hawk 75s and claimed four of them. About the same time another *Schwarm* (a formation of four fighters) was having less success against a

pair of RAF Hurricanes – Leutnant Rudolf Ziegler crashed into a field north of Sedan, probably the victim of another No 73 Sqn ace, Flg Off E J 'Cobber' Kain. Mid-afternoon, the *Gruppe* intercepted a 'low-level' attack on the Sedan bridges and was credited with the destruction of two RAF Battles and six escorting French fighters for the loss of two Bf 109s.

Even I./JG 54 got into the act. After four days of patrolling the quiescent southern sector of the front, which had netted two French fighters for the cost of two aircraft brought down by French anti-aircraft fire in the Luxeuil region, 14 May found Hauptmann von Bonin's *Gruppe* flying escort to a formation of Ju 87 Stukas.

The dive-bombers, tasked with supporting tanks of XIX. *Panzerkorps* as they began the break-out from the Sedan bridgehead, were quickly set upon by a squadron of RAF Hurricanes. In the ensuing engagement, which attracted the attention of two other *Jagdgruppen*, I./JG 54 claimed at least three British fighters destroyed (one described as a 'Spitfire', but all three more likely to have been Hurricanes of No 3 Sqn).

Despite the almost sacrificial efforts on the part of the Allied bomber crews, the Sedan bridgehead could not be contained. The Panzers broke free and the 'race' to the Channel was on, and it could not now be stopped.

The fluid war of movement which followed – the very essence of *Blitzkrieg* – imposed an equally nomadic existence upon the Luftwaffe's short-legged *Jagdgruppen* as they leapfrogged forward across recently occupied territory in an effort to keep pace with the rampaging armour.

On 15 May I./JG 76 left German soil for Bastogne, in Belgium. Twenty-four hours later I./JG 21 moved in to nearby Neufchateau. Although there was something of a lull in aerial activity after the Allies' all-out effort against Sedan, it was on 16 May that I./JG 76 downed a brace of No 85 Sqn Hurricanes over the Luxembourg border. Also on this day I./JG 54, which had resumed its patrolling of the still intact southern reaches of the Maginot Line, lost another machine to Luxeuil's apparently ever vigilant anti-aircraft defences.

The following evening two I./JG 76 pilots were lucky to survive separate brushes with RAF Hurricanes – Leutnant Schulten crash-landed after tangling with No 73 Sqn's 'Cobber' Kain, and Leutnant Schypek bailed out slightly wounded following an attack by a No 615 Sqn fighter.

Further transfers on the central sector saw I./JG 21 and I./JG 76 briefly sharing Charleville before both *Gruppen* moved on again. The former's next stop was an open field near Cambrai. Here, on 22 May, Hauptmann Ultsch's pilots found themselves unexpectedly thrust into the ground-support role. A surprise counter-attack by French tanks, supported by lorried infantry, was developing to the north of the town.

'Red 4' demonstrates the efficacy of the new *hellblau* camouflage scheme – introduced prior to the *Blitzkrieg* in the west – when viewed in its natural setting. Patrolling the summer skies high over France, this machine bears a *'Piepmatz'* ('cheeky sparrow') emblem on its engine cowling, revealing its allegiance to 2./JG 21

The ground-strafing Bf 109s managed to blunt the enemy's advance until Stukas could be called up to complete the job.

I./JG 76 had also moved up to a forward landing ground closer to the coast. It was from here, on 24 May, that it flew its first patrols over the Channel ports of Calais and Boulogne, and – if the pilots' powers of aircraft recognition are to be relied upon – shot down a French Bloch 131 twin-engined bomber.

By this time the British Expeditionary Force (BEF), which had been rushed forward so precipitately into Belgium exactly a fortnight earlier, was in the final throes of a fighting withdrawal to this self-same stretch of French coastline. The BEF's only salvation now lay in evacuation. But even as the bone-weary Allied troops converged on Dunkirk, the Luftwaffe was gathering to try to prevent their escape.

The evacuation began on 26 May, and on this day I./JG 21 transferred to Monchy-Breton, close to St Pol. The common complaint of the British soldiers inside the Dunkirk perimeter and crowding its beaches, 'Where's the bloody RAF?', found no echo among the *Jagdgruppen*. To them the opposition was all too tangible as the tired and battered Hurricanes which had borne the brunt of the French campaign were now joined in the air by fresh Fighter Command units flying from bases in southern England.

I./JG 21's foretaste of the cross-Channel war to come was not encouraging. Within hours of arriving at Monchy-Breton, Feldwebel Harting had been killed and two other pilots had been forced to crash-land machines already damaged beyond repair.

Among the other *Jagdgruppen* transferred to the Dunkirk area was I./JG 54, which had finally been released from months of routine patrolling along the southern stretches of the Maginot Line. To date its opponents had been almost exclusively French. And it was probably the pilots unfamiliarity with the in-line engined machines of Fighter Command which led to their identifying the two fighters claimed at midday on 29 May as 'Curtiss P-40s'.

But there was no mistaking the pair of biplanes the unit downed later that same evening – Fairey Swordfish torpedo-bombers of the Fleet Air Arm (employed over the Channel to counter the E-boat menace during the Dunkirk evacuation). Two of the day's victories – one of each type – were credited to Oberleutnant Hans Schmoller-Haldy, the *Staffelkapitän* of 3./JG 54.

With Holland and Belgium having already surrendered, the withdrawal of the BEF from north-eastern France signalled the end of *'Fall Gelb'*. Now *'Fall Rot'* ('Case Red'), the reduction of the main body of the French Army, could begin. This second stage of the offensive in the west was to be preceded by heavy bombing raids on airfields and other targets in the Greater Paris area on 3 June.

It would be wrong to describe the ensuing campaign as a formality. Fierce fighting still lay ahead. But the

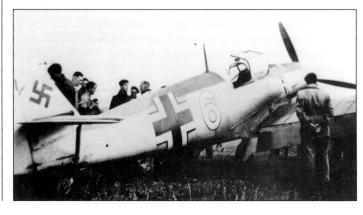

But even blue summer skies can be hazardous, as Unteroffizier Hager of 1./JG 76 found out to his cost on 30 May. He became hopelessly lost while carrying out a routine air test and put down at Orconte, in the Marne Valley – territory still held by the French. Like Hier's machine back in November, 'White 6' was soon sporting *Armée de l'Air* markings (which effectively obliterated the single kill bar seen here on the rudder at the extreme left of the photograph)

In June 1940, with the *Blitzkrieg* in France drawing to a close, the first Iron Crosses, First Class, were awarded. *Gruppenkommandeur* Major Richard Kraut presents the decoration to three stalwarts of his I./JG 76 for their recent achievements. They are, from left to right, Oberleutnant Dietrich Hrabak, Leutnant Hans Philipp and Oberfeldwebel Max Stotz. All three men would go on to far greater things

train of events set in motion at the Meuse crossings had already ensured the ultimate defeat of France. Exactly a fortnight after the bombing of Greater Paris, Marshal Pétain was announcing his appeal for an armistice.

The Luftwaffe, at least, was confident enough to start tidying up its order of battle long before the cease-fire sounded in the west. Upon the outbreak of war the fighter arm, in particular, had still only consisted of a half-formed, heterogeneous collection of incomplete *Geschwader* and semi-autonomous *Gruppen*. Of the 19 *Jagdgruppen* then in existence, less than a third were serving under their parent *Stäbe* (HQ flight). A number of new *Geschwaderstäbe*, including that of JG 54, had been activated during the 'Phoney War' period.

But it was not until the outcome of *'Fall Rot'* was beyond doubt that some semblance of order began to appear in the ranks of the *Jagdwaffe*. Over the next few weeks the motley assortment of individual *Jagdgruppen*, which had been temporarily lumped together to support the *Blitzkrieg* in the west, were gradually redesignated and assigned to permanent *Stäbe*. By the high summer the Luftwaffe fighters were finally organised into nine *Geschwader*, each composed of the standard three *Gruppen*.

One of the first of the 'orphan' *Jagdgruppen* to be reassigned was I./JG 21. On 6 June 1940, after having claimed 37 kills while subordinated to JG 27 during the recent campaigning in the Low Countries and France, Hauptmann Fritz Ultsch's East Prussians became the III. *Gruppe* of *Jagdgeschwader* 54.

Just over a week later the Austrians of Oberstleutnant Kraut's I./JG 76 were withdrawn from the fighting around Orléans and redesignated as JG 54's II. *Gruppe*.

Meanwhile the Franconian I./JG 54 under Hauptmann von Bonin had been covering the advance west of Paris. The *Gruppe's* last casualty of the French campaign occurred during a dogfight over Evreux on 14 June. But its next victories, claimed nine days later, would be scored over Holland.

For on 21 June, while French troops were still grimly holding out along some parts of the Maginot Line, the 'brand new' JG 54 had been transferred in its entirety back to the Dutch coastal belt.

Another member of the *Gruppe* to receive the award in June, for his five victories to date, was Lt Anton Stangl. Unlike the trio above, however, the days of Stangl's operational career were already numbered. With the Battle of France effectively won, the Battle of Britain was about to begin. And Oberleutnant Anton Stangl would be one of the 35 pilots of the newly-formed JG 54 reported killed, missing or captured during the 'official' course of the coming Battle

THE BATTLE OF BRITAIN – BEFORE AND AFTER

Withdrawn from France before the last shot had been fired, JG 54 was now tasked with defending newly-occupied Holland against incursions by the RAF from across the North Sea. To discharge this duty Major Mettig's three *Gruppen* were dispersed on six airfields.

In the west of the country, closest to the border with Belgium, II./JG 54 was based at Vlissingen (Flushing) on the island of Walcheren, in the Scheldt Estuary, and at Rotterdam-Waalhaven. I./JG 54 occupied Eindhoven, also close to the Belgian frontier but further inland, and Amsterdam-Schiphol. Lastly, III./JG 54 were deployed on fields situated on either side of Amsterdam – at Soesterberg to the south, and at Bergen aan Zee which, as its name implies, lay on the coast to the north.

Within little more than 48 hours of their arrival in the Netherlands, pilots of I. *Gruppe* were in action. 3. *Staffel's* Leutnant Adolf Kinzinger and Unteroffizier Adolf Strohauer were each credited with a Blenheim on the evening of 23 June (possibly the two No 107 Sqn aircraft which reportedly crashed in Holland on that date).

Three days later Oberleutnant Hans von Schmoller-Haldy, the *Staffelkapitän* of 3./JG 54, had a lucky escape after intercepting another Blenheim near Rotterdam. Hit by return fire from the bomber's dorsal turret, a wounded von Schmoller-Haldy nevertheless managed to bring off a shaky landing. He was extricated from his machine, which had nosed over, and rushed to hospital. His injury would keep him off flying for the next month.

Those same four weeks were to see the opening moves in what was to become the Battle of Britain, as Luftwaffe units based in France began to attack shipping in the English Channel. Meanwhile, for JG 54 in the Netherlands it was a period of mixed fortunes. On 27 June the *Geschwader* claimed at least four more Blenheims, including a

Before taking station in the Pas de Calais, JG 54 was first tasked with the defence of German-occupied Holland. The new III./JG 54 (ex-I./JG 21) was deployed in the Amsterdam area. The *Emil* in the foreground, believed to be a machine of the *Stabsschwarm*, sports the *Gruppe* badge on its cowling . . .

brace for Hauptmann von Bonin, *Kommandeur* of I. *Gruppe*. But on 8 July two Bf 109s crashed into Rotterdam harbour basin – possibly as the result of a mid-air collision – and an NCO pilot of 2. *Staffel* was drowned.

The RAF was also targeting the airfields occupied by JG 54. Four groundcrew were killed, and others injured, when Bergen was attacked on 15 July, and II. *Gruppe* sustained further losses in men and material when Soesterberg was hit during a raid on the night of 23-24 July. In between alarms such as these the *Geschwader* was occasionally called upon to escort the Junkers Ju 52 VIP transports of the Führer's Special Flight whenever Adolf Hitler, as C-in-C of the *Wehrmacht*, or members of his entourage undertook tours of inspection (a service also previously provided by I./JG 76 during the recent campaign in France).

The closing weeks of July had been marked by an intensification of the air war over the Channel to the west. The brief pause which then followed at the beginning of August was brought about by the Luftwaffe's need to regroup for the all-out aerial offensive against southern England which was to pave the way for seaborne invasion. As part of the build-up of forces being assembled for the coming onslaught, JG 54 was ordered to vacate its Dutch bases and take up station in the Pas de Calais.

During the first week of August the *Geschwader* began transferring to the three well camouflaged, but still somewhat 'underdeveloped', forward landing grounds south of Calais to which they had been assigned. Major Mettig's *Geschwaderstab*, together with I. *Gruppe* under Hauptmann von Bonin, were based at Campagne-les-Guines, about ten miles (16 km) inland from the coast.

With 4./JG 54 having suffered severe losses after being caught in an RAF bombing raid while taking off from Holland on 7 August, a depleted II. *Gruppe*, commanded since 11 July by Hauptmann Winterer, settled in at Hermelinghen, some three miles (5 km) further to the south. Hauptmann Ultsch's III. *Gruppe* found itself in 'a pasture so criss-crossed by sheep-tracks that new pilots nearly always came to grief at the moment of take-off'. Although often referred to as Guines-South, this field was, in fact, situated to the north of *Geschwader* HQ, lying between Campagne and the port of Calais.

As one of the first units to arrive in the Pas de Calais, 1. *Staffel* had also been among the first to see action against RAF Fighter Command over the Channel. One the morning of 5 August a pilot of 1./JG 54 had forced-landed back in France after a brush with Spitfires off the Kent coast. That same afternoon the *Staffel* had escorted a small formation of Ju 88 bombers sent to attack a convoy in the Straits of Dover.

Engaged by a squadron of Hurricanes, *Staffelkapitän* Oberleutnant Reinhard Seiler was hit, and although severely wounded, he was able to take to his parachute. 'Seppl' Seiler was rescued from mid-Channel a few hours later by a German naval vessel, but would not return to operations until the following spring.

By 10 August the majority of the *Geschwader*, with the exception of the unfortunate 4. *Staffel*, was established in France. Located on fields only a few miles apart, and subordinated to *Jafü* 2 – the fighter command charged with ensuring Luftwaffe air superiority over south-east England – *Jagdgeschwader* 54's three component *Gruppen* were at last about to commence operations as a single, unified force.

. . . as does this Bf 109E-4 of 9. *Staffel's* Leutnant Josef Eberle who, despite being wounded, made it back across the Channel before putting his 'Yellow 13' down on its belly in France on 12 August. Although the previous *hellblau* finish is now being toned down by overspraying, note the bright yellow (or white?) tips to the wings, tailplanes and upper rudder segment of Eberle's E-4

But there were some who would not enjoy the novel experience for long. 11 August was occupied by a series of *Freie Jagd* (free-ranging fighter sweeps) sorties over the Dover-Canterbury area of Kent. More of the same were scheduled for the morning and evening of the following day. In between these latter, elements of the *Geschwader* were ordered to provide the fighter escort for a bombing raid on 'Canterbury airfield' (presumably Manston) in the late afternoon.

Among those taking off from Guines-South for this 12 August mission was Oberleutnant Albrecht Drefl of the *Gruppenstab* III./JG 54;

'In the dogfight which developed (close to the target) at an altitude of some 6000 m (19,500 ft) I managed to shoot down a Spitfire, but was myself shot down shortly afterwards. Fortunately, my machine did not catch fire, but the engine and propeller pitch mechanism had been hit and everything stopped. I had to make a belly landing.'

Wounded by splinters, Drefl set his fighter down in a field near Margate. After retrieving his *Jabuko* (pilot's overnight case) from behind his seat, he was taken to the local hospital where he was to spend 'several days' recovering before embarking upon his PoW career proper. Another member of III. *Gruppe* had been less fortunate. Gefreiter Stabner's machine went into the sea off the Kent coast. Three more pilots were wounded during the day's actions but managed to nurse their damaged aircraft back to France. In addition to the Spitfire mentioned by Drefl, at least one other was claimed, by 2. *Staffel's* Feldwebel Alfred Schunk.

The next morning was to see the launch of the much vaunted '*Adlerangriff*' ('Eagle Assault'), the all-out attack which was aimed at nothing less than the complete annihilation of RAF Fighter Command and its bases in southern England. But a combination of poor weather and a disastrous breakdown in communications quickly turned '*Adlertag*' ('Eagle Day') into a shambles.

In some places bomber formations set out across the Channel without their fighter escorts. Elsewhere, fighter units flew to England on their own, minus the bombers they were supposed to be protecting! One of the main reasons for JG 54's recent transfer from Holland to France had been to add their weight to the '*Adlerangriff*' operations. As it transpired, the *Geschwader's* participation in the events of that disastrous 13 August was minimal. Its contribution is best summed up by the three-word entry in the log-book of one II. *Gruppe* pilot – '*Freie Jagd* – aborted'.

On 15 August, however, JG 54 was back over Kent in force. All three *Gruppen* were involved in this day's actions, which included both *Freie Jagd* and bomber escort missions. The price they paid was four pilots killed or missing. 9. *Staffel's* Unteroffizier Niedermeier was shot down near Cranbrook, Leutnant Gerlach and Unteroffizier Hautkappe, of 2. and 5./JG 54 respectively, both disappeared over the Channel, and Feldwebel Schnaar, also of 2. *Staffel*, limped back to France in his crippled fighter, only to lose his life when he crashed at Courtrai. In addition, there were two fatalities among the ground personnel after an incident at Guines-South. The single Spitfire claimed by 1. *Staffel's* Feldwebel Schönweiss was poor recompense.

Over the course of the next ten days there was a slow but steady trickle of attrition among the *Geschwader's* men and machines. On 16 August Feldwebel Knedler of 3./JG 54 failed to return from a cross-Channel operation, and a wounded Unteroffizier Rimmel wrote off his aircraft in a forced-landing at St Inglevert. Forty-eight hours later, during the 'Hardest Day' of the entire Battle, JG 54's material losses amounted to just three fighters damaged – a 7. *Staffel* machine which crashed on take-off from Guines, and two II. *Gruppe* E-3s that were hit during an evening raid on Vlissingen by Blenheims of Fighter Command.

On 21 August a III. *Gruppe Emil* was a total loss after yet another take-off crash from Guines (those sheep-tracks were still doing their stuff!), while an E-1 of 6. *Staffel* sustained lesser damage belly-landing back at Vlissingen. The next day two 5. *Staffel* NCOs were killed when a Gotha Go 145 hack of II. *Gruppe* came down while on a domestic flight. And two days after that another communications machine – this time an Arado Ar 66 of the *Geschwaderstab* – was destroyed at Amsterdam-Schiphol when Blenheims again bombed airfields in Holland.

By now it was all too apparent to the Luftwaffe High Command that the *'Adlerangriff'* offensive had failed dismally. Far from being eliminated, enemy fighter opposition appeared to be growing stronger. Hermann Göring cast around for scapegoats. Ignoring the real reasons for what he perceived to be his *Jagdwaffe's* 'failure', he lit upon the fighter arm's *Geschwaderkommodore*. They were all too old, he declared, and lacked the necessary aggression. They would have to go.

In some respects the portly *Reichsmarschall* was right. Several of his unit commanders were, like himself, ex-World War 1 flyers unsuited to lead modern fighters in combat. Henceforth, the Luftwaffe C-in-C decreed,

Another 12 August casualty was this Bf 109E-4 of the *Gruppe's* Technical Officer, Oberleutnant Albrecht Drefl. Close inspection reveals a cluster of 0.303-inch bullet holes on, and close alongside, the *Gruppe* badge. If the opposing Spitfire pilot was using it as a target, he could not have wished for a neater bull! His marksmanship resulted in this equally neat belly-landing at Hengrove, near Margate, on 12 August

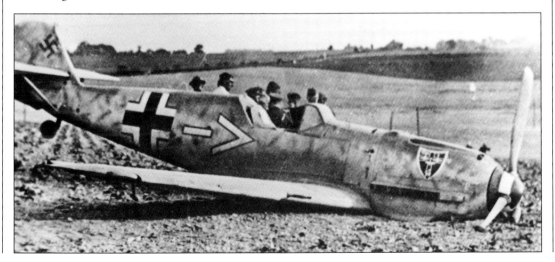

no *Geschwaderkommodore* was to be more than 32 years of age. What he required were younger, more dynamic pilots who had displayed their courage and leadership skills in the recent campaigns against France and the Low Countries.

Although too young to have flown in World War 1, JG 54's Major Martin Mettig, at 37, was an automatic candidate for replacement – even if he had not already been deemed the 'wrong temperament' for a fighter pilot by higher authority. Whether by luck or good judgement, the officer selected to take Mettig's place at the head of JG 54 was an inspired choice. He would immediately stamp his imprint upon the *Geschwader*, lead it for almost three years, and remain indissolubly linked with it thereafter.

Twenty-eight-year-old Hans 'Hannes' Trautloft was the archetypal officer Göring was seeking to inject 'a new spirit' into his frontline fighter units. After taking civil flying lessons, he had joined the *Reichswehr* in late 1932. He was among the select early few to be trained at the secret military flying school established by the *Reichswehr*, in agreement with the Russians, at Lipezk north of Voronezh in the USSR.

Promoted to leutnant on 1 January 1934, Hannes Trautloft then in turn spent time instructing at various fighter training establishments, before fighting in Spain with the *Legion Condor*, where he was credited with five victories.

The outbreak of World War 2 saw Oberleutnant Trautloft serving as *Staffelkapitän* of 2./JG 77, with whom he scored one kill in Poland. On 22 September 1939 he became *Kommandeur* of I./JG 20 (another of the semi-autonomous *Jagdgruppen* on the Luftwaffe order of battle upon the outbreak of hostilities, and which was to be redesignated III./JG 51 in July 1940). During the recent campaign in the Low Countries and France, the now Hauptmann Trautloft had added five more victories to his list of kills. This then was the man who, on 25 August 1940, replaced Major Martin Mettig as *Kommodore* of *Jagdgeschwader* 54.

Although not a high scorer himself, Hannes Trautloft combined his undoubted ability as a fighter pilot in the air with that even more valuable quality – the gift of natural leadership. For him, the well-being of his men, and the success of the *Geschwader* as a whole, counted for more than personal prowess and aggrandisement.

It was typical of Trauloft that one of his first thoughts should be to instil a sense of unity into his three 'provincial *Gruppen*' by introducing a common *Geschwader* badge. For inspiration he turned to his own roots. He had been born in Gross-Obingen, a few miles north of Weimar. The latter city was the state capital of Thuringia, an area which was known as the 'Green Heart of Germany'. As soon as operational commitments allowed, every one of the JG 54's aircraft and vehicles would be emblazoned with a simple, but striking 'Green Heart'.

Retaining their own individual *Gruppen* (and often *Staffel*) insignia

The man whose name was to become indissolubly linked with JG 54, Hauptmann Hannes Trautloft, was appointed *Kommodore* on 25 August 1940. Seen here (centre) smoking a rustic pipe rather than his more habitual cigar, Trautloft is flanked by his *Geschwader* Adjutant Oberleutnant Otto Kath (left) and Technical Officer Oberleutnant Pichon Kalau von Hofe (right)

too, JG 54's fighters would subsequently provide some of the most colourfully heraldic machines to be seen in the entire *Jagdwaffe*. In return, and as a tribute to the varied backgrounds of those under his command, Trautloft's own aircraft – and those of many who flew in his *Stabsschwarm* – would bear the 'Green Heart' with the three *Gruppe* badges superimposed in miniature.

But all this lay in the future. The present reality was the cross-Channel war with the RAF in which JG 54 was becoming increasingly embroiled. On the very day Hauptmann Trautloft assumed command, I. *Gruppe's* Oberleutnant Held was killed in combat (with a Spitfire of No 54 Sqn) while flying an evening *Freie Jagd* over Dover. Leutnant Siegfried von Matuschka of 2. *Staffel* evened the score by claiming another Spitfire (also possibly a No 54 Sqn machine) during the same mission.

Further losses would be suffered in the weeks ahead. On 28 August 1. *Staffel's* Feldwebel Otto Schöttle crashed in flames following a dogfight over Dungeness, but survived to become a PoW. Unteroffizier Kleemann of II. *Gruppe* was not so lucky. His *Emil* disappeared over mid-Channel.

Forty-eight hours later II./JG 54's Oberleutnant Roth and Leutnant Rudolf 'Rudi' Ziegler (who had opened the *Gruppe's* scoreboard over Poland a year ago almost to the day) both became prisoners after colliding with each other while 'attacking an English plane' over Surrey. On 1 September Oberleutnant Anton Stangl, *Staffelkapitän* of 5./JG 54, followed them into captivity when he suffered the same fate.

5. *Staffel* had been split up during a bomber escort mission to Tilbury docks on that first morning of September. Flying with his wingman, Stangl spotted a Spitfire some 2500 ft (750 m) below. Before diving to the attack, he automatically glanced over his left shoulder to make sure there was nothing on his tail. It was as well that he did, for what he saw was;

'. . . another Messerschmitt of an unknown unit, some 50 or 60 metres (160-200 ft) away, heading straight for me at full speed with its propeller disc shining in the sun. That look saved my life.'

Although realising that a collision was unavoidable, Stangl instinctively pushed the stick forward, yanking it to the right as he did so. The nose of his aircraft went down. But not enough. The propeller blades of the other fighter struck the cowling just ahead of Stangl's cockpit. He was thrown forward and blacked out momentarily when he smashed his head on the Revi gunsight. Quickly coming to, he discovered that his port wing was gone ('I had the best view out of a plane in my entire life at that moment!'), but once again ingrained training took over and he prepared to bail out.

Fortunately, his stricken 'Black 14' had gone into an outside spin and he had no difficulty in getting out of the cockpit. In fact, he was 'thrown out with terrible force'. He opened his parachute at about 19,500 ft (6000 m) and, in the half-hour it took him to reach the ground, even found time to admire the view;

Throughout much of the Battle of Britain JG 54 also maintained small detachments in Holland for local coastal defence duties. 5. *Staffel's* 'Black 4' (possibly Wk-Nr 3639) was operated by one such *Kommando*, and its present predicament – on a beach near the Scheldt Estuary – was not the result of enemy action, but of engine failure. This photograph was taken in the early evening light of 26 August 1940

'Visibility was excellent that day. I could see the whole width of the English Channel and beyond. On the one side the headland of Dungeness. On the other, Calais, and – a few kilometres inland – the unmistakable patch of woods bordering our improvised airfield!'

Twenty-four hours after Stangl's involuntary descent straight into a British army barracks near Ashford, in Kent, JG 54 suffered one of its worst days of the entire Battle. On 2 September a pair of II. *Gruppe* pilots, Oberleutnant Elsing and Unteroffizier Frauendorf, were killed in yet another mid-air collision, this time near Calais while returning from an operational mission.

Very much a victim of the Battle, Unteroffizier Heinrich Elbers' *Emil* crash-landed near Ashford after an encounter with RAF Hurricanes on 2 September. Like many of its kind, this machine of 8./JG 54 was later put on display to raise money for the local war effort. Note the unusual position of the numeral beneath the windscreen – a feature of many III. *Gruppe* machines at this period – and the hole in the cowling where somebody has already 'liberated' the unit badge as a souvenir

On the same day III./JG 54 lost two of its numbers over Kent – Oberleutnant Ekkehard Schelcher of the *Gruppenstab* crashed southwest of Canterbury (his remains would not be discovered for almost 40 years), and 8. *Staffel's* Unteroffizier Heinrich Elbers was captured after a spectacular crash-landing close to Ashford. Two other III. *Gruppe* aircraft sustained serious damage in forced-landings back in France.

After the single loss of Oberleutnant Witt of 3./JG 54 off Dover on 4 September, another black day was to follow. The 5th saw three more pilots killed and a fourth posted missing. The latter was I. *Gruppe's* Unteroffizier Fritz Hotzelmann, who parachuted into captivity when his machine was hit in a low-level dogfight over Maidstone.

The three fatalities all occurred on the Essex side of the Thames Estuary. Unteroffizier Behse and Feldwebel Dettler, of 5. and 9. *Staffeln* respectively, came down into the sea off Southend and on Pitsea Marshes. The third casualty was Hauptmann Fritz Ultsch, the *Gruppenkommandeur* of III./JG 54, whose *Emil* was shot down by a No 17 Sqn Hurricane, also close to Pitsea. It was after this action that *Kommodore* Hannes Trautloft famously remarked, 'The sky was full of roundels. For the first time we had the definite feeling that we were outnumbered'.

Under such circumstances, and given the *Geschwader's* recent loss rate, it is perhaps not surprising that a certain Leutnant Hans-Hellmuth Ostermann noted the increased tension amongst his fellow 7. *Staffel* pilots back at Guines as they began openly to talk, for the first time, of a 'posting to a quieter base'.

In fact, the worst of the Battle was over for JG 54. Further casualties would inevitably be sustained before the year was out. However, with the first bloody month in the Pas de Calais now behind them, the *Geschwader's* fortunes began to change as experience grew, personalities emerged, and their own scores started to climb.

After the death of Fritz Ultsch, future *Experte* Oberleutnant Günther Scholz was named as acting *Kommandeur* of III. *Gruppe*. Scholz, who had previously headed the seemingly somewhat dispirited 7./JG 54, was the second *Staffelkapitän* to be elevated to the command of a *Gruppe* at this time. Exactly one week earlier, on 30 August, an informal party had been held in Hermelinghen's small village school – now serving as the officer's

Very occasionally the boot was on the other foot. This Spitfire (X4260 XT-D of No 603 Sqn), flown by Plt Off J L Caister, reportedly chased a gaggle of Bf 109s back across the Channel on 6 September, only to be forced down by Hauptmann Hubertus von Bonin, *Kommandeur* of I./JG 54, close to the *Gruppe's* base at Campagne-les-Guines (see *Osprey Aircraft of the Aces 11 - Bf 109D/E Aces 1939-41*, page 77, for further details)

mess of II./JG 54 – to celebrate the recent appointment of 4. *Staffel's* Hauptmann Dietrich Hrabak as the new *Gruppenkommandeur* in place of Hauptmann Winterer.

On 9 September, when Hrabak's *Gruppe* escorted a formation of He 111 bombers against London, and claimed three Spitfires without loss while so doing, another pair of I. *Gruppe Emils* disappeared over the Channel. 1. *Staffel's* Feldwebel Biber was reported missing, but the other (unnamed) pilot of 3./JG 54 was recovered by the German *Seenotdienst* (air-sea rescue service). Nine days later an anonymous 1. *Staffel* pilot was also plucked safely from the Channel by this same overworked, but nevertheless efficient organisation.

In the interim, the historic 15 September had been and gone. The ferocious air battles fought on this date have since come to be regarded as the climax of the whole campaign and, in the United Kingdom, are now commemorated annually as 'Battle of Britain Day'.

For the pilots of JG 54, the operations of 15 September had proved a frustrating and unrewarding experience. Tethered closely – by special edict of the *Reichsmarschall* – to the bombers they were escorting, they had been strictly forbidden to patrol freely at a distance around and, more importantly, above their charges (another example of Göring's failure to grasp the practicalities of modern aerial warfare). The *Geschwader's* pilots could therefore do little more than juggle their throttles in frantic efforts to keep station with the sluggish bomber formations as British fighters dived and swooped upon them almost unmolested.

It was only the enemy fighters' concentrating on the more lucrative bomber targets which prevented JG 54 from suffering severe losses. One III. *Gruppe* machine did very nearly come to grief, but was saved by the skill and ingenuity of its pilot.

The *Emil* of Oberleutnant Hans-Ekkehard Bob took a cannon shell in the radiator over Canterbury. From his present altitude of 12,000 ft

9. *Staffel's* Oberleutnant Hans-Ekkehard Bob, who famously 'roller-coasted' back to France with an overheating engine on 15 September. Pictured here at a later date (note the Knight's Cross awarded on 7 March 1941), Bob clowns in the cockpit of his 'Yellow 1' – he can hardly be returning from an operational sortie dressed in a leather greatcoat!

More proof that the cross-Channel traffic was not all one-way. Hptm Hannes Trautloft (right) and members of his *Geschwaderstab* attempt to converse with the diminutive, and obviously dejected, observer of a shot down Bomber Command Blenheim

A line-up of 8. *Staffel Emils*, still wearing their basic *hellblau* finish, are seen at Guines-South in September. The pilot of the machine in the foreground (with two kill bars on its rudder) is unknown, but 'Black 3' behind it was the regular mount of Leutnant Erwin Leykauf

(3600 m), Bob knew only too well that to switch off his engine and glide would get him no further than mid-Channel at most. But without coolant, the engine, if left running, would quickly overheat and seize completely. So he decided to combine the two options open to him.

When the engine was near to boiling he cut the motor, sacrificing precious altitude in a shallow glide until the airflow from the windmilling propeller had cooled the engine sufficiently for it to be restarted. Repeating this process several times, Bob's flight took on all the characteristics of a roller-coaster ride. But the ploy got him safely back to France.

Although the attention of the entire population of southern England was focused, somewhat understandably, on the action ranging overhead as RAF fighters sought to defend their airspace from near constant Luftwaffe attack, the offensive activity across the Channel and North Sea was not all one-way. Throughout the Battle, Bomber Command had been striking back, raiding ports along the German-occupied coast and targeting airfields in France and the Low Countries.

To help combat this menace, all three *Gruppen* of JG 54 had, for some time, been deploying detachments (usually in *Schwarm* strength) to a number of Dutch airfields. Now, in the last week of September, I./JG 54 was withdrawn completely from the Pas de Calais and transferred to the north German coastal belt.

Hauptmann von Bonin's *Gruppenstab* was headquartered at Jever, with his individual *Staffeln* dispersed in a wide arc from the Danish border down to Holland. Among the bases they would occupy over the course of the next eight months would be Westerland, on the island of Sylt, Wangerooge (another island in the Frisian chain), Wesermünde and Groningen, in the Netherlands.

Meanwhile, to replace the departing I. *Gruppe*, II./JG 54 had vacated Hermelinghen on 22 September, making the short hop northwards to

operate alongside the *Geschwader-stab* at Campagne. In the eight days that were left of September four more pilots would fail to return. On 23 September Oberfeld-webel Knippscheer of 3. *Staffel* was reported missing after parachuting into the Channel off Dover (he would be I./JG 54's last casualty of the Battle).

On 27 September – a busy day for the remaining *Gruppen* of the *Geschwader*, with some pilots flying as many as four separate sorties, including two round trips escorting bombers to London – 8. *Staffel's*

Offering a good close-up of 8./JG 54's *'Piepmatz'* emblem, this photograph shows the DB 601 engine of a yellow-cowlinged Bf 109 coughing protestingly into life as the mechanic on the wingroot reaches into the cockpit to ease back the throttle. The 'black man' on the far side, his work done, removes the starter handle

Oberleutnant Anton Schon was killed when he hit a fence while trying to put his crippled fighter down near Faversham. Finally, on the last day of the month, Unteroffizier Wilhelm Braatz of 9./JG 54 lost his life in a crash east of Tonbridge, in Kent, and 7. *Staffel's* Feldwebel Marcke forced-landed and was captured close to Bexhill, on the Sussex coast.

By a quirk of fate, the first two of October's nine losses were likewise pilots from 9. and 7. *Staffeln*, brought down on the same day (the 9th) following action against RAF fighters, and with similar results – 9./JG 54's Leutnant Josef Eberle disappeared over the Channel, but Oberfeldwebel Fritz Schweser of 7. *Staffel* was taken prisoner after forced-landing near Hawkinge.

Seventy-two hours later another two pilots were lost in very similar circumstances. This time it was 7. *Staffel* which suffered the fatality, Leutnant Friedrich Behrens being presumed shot down over the Channel, whereas Leutnant Bernhard Malischewski, who was a member of the *Gruppenstab* II./JG 54, survived both an encounter with legendary RAF ace Flt Lt 'Bob' Stanford Tuck, and the subsequent forced-landing near Tenterden, to enter captivity.

On 20 October, during a morning *Freie Jagd* along the Kent coast, 9. *Staffel's* Feldwebel Adolf Iburg was almost as fortunate to escape his brush with another of Fighter Command's top scorers – Flt Lt A A

The last three of the 18 kill bars seen here on the rudder of Oberleutnant Hans Philipp's *Emil* were all claimed on 13 October. Two more would win the *StaKa* of 4./JG 54 (pictured second left) the *Geschwader's* second Knight's Cross on 2 November. On the left Oberleutnant Pichon Kalau von Hofe, whose current tally then stood at four kills

'Archie' McKellar – only slightly wounded and still able to pull off a forced-landing close to New Romney.

On 21 October JG 54 was awarded its first Knight's Cross. The recipient was Hauptmann Dietrich Hrabak, *Kommandeur* of II. *Gruppe*. With his overall score then standing at 16, Hrabak was the 24th member of the *Jagdwaffe* to receive the decoration during the Battle of Britain. The following day one of his *Staffelkapitäne*, Oberleutnant Hans Philipp of 4./JG 54, was similarly honoured for having achieved 20 victories (including a treble on 13 October) since his first kill over Poland more than 13 months earlier.

By this time the outcome of the daylight battle over southern England had long been conceded. The Luftwaffe bombers were operating more and more under cover of darkness. A furious Göring, anxious not to lose face – and needing to be able to show evidence of some sort of continued offensive by day – had therefore ordered that a third of his Channel-based fighters should be converted to carry bombs. For most *Jagdgruppen* this meant designating one *Staffel* to undertake *Jabo* (fighter-bomber) missions, leaving the other two to provide fighter escort.

It was during just such operations that the *Geschwader* was to suffer its next two losses. On 25 October the *Jabos* of 4./JG 54 mounted at least two separate attacks against the Greater London area. The results of the raids are not known, but two pilots of the escorting 5. *Staffel* failed to return. Oberleutnant Joachim Schypek and Leutnant Ernst Wagner both forced-landed in Kent.

Two days later, October's final casualty was also III./JG 54's last loss of the Battle. During a morning *Freie Jagd* over Kent, Unteroffizier Arno Zimmermann's 7. *Staffel Emil* was caught by RAF fighters. His engine severely damaged, Zimmermann belly-landed on the beach near Dungeness. Meanwhile, on the other side of the Channel, the rest of the *Gruppe* was in the throes of vacating Guines-South and transferring back

Forced down almost intact near Tenterden, in Kent, by Flt Lt Bob Stanford Tuck on 12 October, this machine of *Gruppenstab* II./JG 54 is quickly camouflaged to prevent it being shot up on the ground by other Luftwaffe fighters. While pilot Leutnant Bernhard Malischewski entered captivity, his *Emil* was subsequently taken on tour . . .

. . . getting as far north as Lincoln, where it was the prize exhibit in the city's War Weapons Week

Another II. *Gruppe* machine downed over Kent in October was Oberleutnant Joachim Schypek's 'Red 7'. Despite that rear-view mirror, he was unable to escape an attack from astern by RAF fighters south-west of Ashford, and was forced to land when his engine seized (note that only two of the propeller blades are bent). Like Malischewski's *Emil*, this aircraft also displays a dark rectangle below the windscreen – in preparation for a *Gruppe* badge perhaps?

to the Dutch airfields of Schiphol, Katwijk, De Kooy and Hastede.

With two of his *Gruppen* now defending the North Sea coastline (I./JG 54 under *Luftgaukommando XI* in northern Germany, and III./JG 54 a part of *Luftgaukommando Holland*), Hannes Trautloft's *Geschwaderstab* had just Hauptmann Dietrich Hrabak's II. *Gruppe* in attendance at Campagne to continue the cross-Channel offensive.

But with the British regarding the Battle as already over and won, and winter beginning to close in, the Luftwaffe's daylight activities were ebbing fast. Few missions penetrated far inland, and all five of II./JG 54's November casualties were reported missing over the sea.

Leutnant Otto Grothe of 4./JG 54 went down off the Kent coast on the second day of the month. Almost a fortnight later, on 15 November, the same *Staffel's* Oberfeldwebel Karl Hier (who had inadvertently presented the French with an intact Bf 109 back in November 1939, but who had been released from captivity at the close of the campaign in France) disappeared into the sea off Shoeburyness. Two members of 5./JG 54 were also lost over the Thames Estuary on 17 November – Oberfeldwebel Wilhelm Donninger and *Staffelkapitän* Oberleutnant Roloff von Aspern.

The last casualty of all was Obergefreiter Simon Helmberger of Hrabak's *Gruppenstab*, who failed to return from a sortie on 23 November. Within a week II./JG 54 would also be under orders to retire from the Pas de Calais. It transferred to Delmenhorst, near Bremen, on 3 December. The following day III. *Gruppe* ended its six-week stay in Holland when the unit also returned to the Reich, taking up winter quarters at Dortmund.

Although JG 54's participation in the Battle of Britain had not lasted as long as that of many of the other *Jagdgeschwader* involved – it had not arrived in the Pas de Calais until August, and two of its *Gruppen* had been withdrawn early to take up defensive duties elsewhere – the cross-Channel campaign had cost it dear.

Between 12 August and 1 December no fewer than 43 pilots had been reported killed, missing or captured – a casualty rate of close on 40 per cent, or the equivalent of more than an entire *Gruppe*. Of course, some component units were hit harder than others. When the *Kapitän* of 3./JG 54, Oberleutnant Hans Schmoller-Haldy, left Campagne for northern Germany on 27 September, it is said that the '*Staffel*' had comprised just himself and his wingman, Leutnant Adolf Kinzinger!

Despite the severity of such losses, they were far outweighed by the number of victories claimed. Some sources credit JG 54 with almost 240 kills during the Battle. But, on the premise that the average score of a *Jagdgruppe* taking part in the Battle of Britain was between 50 and 60, this total seems unsustainable (although the combined score for III./JG 54 has been given as 67). Perhaps the discrepancy lies in the number of claims first submitted, as opposed to those officially credited – there are instances of some pilots having half their initial claims subsequently disallowed.

Forty-eight hours after Joachim Schypek's capture, 7. *Staffel's* Unteroffizier Arno Zimmermann suffered the same fate. Also nursing a damaged engine, Zimmermann put his 'White 13' down on the shingle near Dungeness on 27 October. Although barely visible here, this machine carries its individual numeral below the windscreen, and sports 7./JG 54's 'Winged clog' badge on its yellow cowling

Long before the Battle ended, I./JG 54 had been withdrawn from France to resume its North Sea coastal defence duties – individual *Staffeln* and *Schwärme* were deployed on airfields in Holland and northern Germany. The unmistakable silhouette of a twin-funnelled ocean liner in the background (right) would suggest that this snow-covered expanse, pictured in the winter of 1940-41, is Wesermünde, close by the commercial port of Bremerhaven

Whatever the true figures, it appears beyond doubt that JG 54 achieved many more successes than losses suffered. Although the *Geschwader* did not produce the likes of a Mölders, Galland, Oesau or Wick during the course of the Battle, it did have several pilots with scores well into double figures.

In addition to the two already mentioned, JG 54 received a third Knight's Cross in 1940. But Oberleutnant Arnold Lignitz, whose receipt of the award was announced on 5 November, had taken over command of III. *Gruppe* from acting *Kommandeur* Günther Scholz only the day before, and all 19 of his victories to date had been scored while flying with III./JG 51.

The vast majority, however, including two *Staffelkapitäne*, had achieved all their kills while serving in the units which now made up JG 54. The resourceful Oberleutnant Hans-Ekkehard Bob of 9. *Staffel*, for example, claimed his 19th on 11 November (although he would have to wait nearly four months for his Knight's Cross). And 5. *Staffel's* Oberleutnant Roloff von Aspern had scored at least 18 before being posted missing. Many more, at present with perhaps only two or three victories to their name, were nonetheless on the first rung of the ladder to future success. For JG 54's time, and place, was yet to come.

Between their withdrawal from the Channel front and the end of 1940, all three *Gruppen* made good their losses in men and machines. In this they were greatly assisted by the *Ergänzungsstaffel*, which had been established at Katwijk in October. In contrast to the RAF, whose trainee aircrew, upon completion of their flight schooling, were pooled in an operational training unit before being posted to whichever frontline squadron happened then to be in need of replacements, each Luftwaffe *Geschwader* was provided with its own *Ergänzungsstaffel* (literally, 'supplementary squadron').

These served, in effect, as 'in-house' Operational Training Units (OTU), readying trainees for service with one of the combat *Staffeln*. As the requirement for replacements increased, the early *Ergänzungs-staffeln* were quickly enlarged into *Ergänzungsgruppen*, Erg.St/JG 54, for example, being redesignated Erg.Gr./JG 54 in February 1941. Later still, these individual, unit-specific *Ergänzungsgruppen*, were all amalgamated into autonomous

Ergänzungsgeschwader. Supplying replacement pilots for the whole of the *Jagdwaffe*, the EJGs thus became the direct equivalent of the RAF's OTUs.

The winter months of 1940-41 also provided the surviving pilots of JG 54 with a much-needed break. Group skiing holidays were organised in the Austrian resort of Kitzbühel – very much a 'home away from home' for the members if II./JG 54, but presumably more of a novelty for the others, especially those more familiar with the lowland lakes of East Prussia!

This idyll did not last for long. On 15 January 1941 Hannes Trautloft's *Geschwaderstab*, together with II. and III. *Gruppen*, were ordered back to France. Based at Le Mans, with forward detachments operating out of Cherbourg, they spent the next two months augmenting the aerial defence of Normandy. It proved to be a relatively undemanding task, as is reflected in the fact that only two fighters were lost – neither of them, it is believed, to enemy action.

On 14 February 9./JG 54's Unteroffizier Karl Albrecht crashed in Belgium during a domestic flight. Just under a month later, on 12 March, an E-4/B of 4. *Staffel* failed to return from a routine patrol. It was being piloted by the same Simon Helmberger who had been reported missing back in November just as II. *Gruppe* were retiring from the Pas de Calais. Presumably rescued from the Channel, he had since caught up with the unit in the Homeland. But the now Unteroffizier Helmberger would not be lucky a second time.

On 29 March the *Gruppens*' brief period of service in Normandy came to a close. They were on the move again, and now their course was taking them south-eastwards.

Early in 1941 II. *Gruppe* began applying a unique three-tone 'crazy-paving' camouflage scheme to its *Emils*. The new finish is modelled here by two sister-ships of 6. *Staffel* – 'Yellow 11', being refuelled from a Luftwaffe bowser . . .

. . . and 'Yellow 10', an E-4/B (note ventral bomb rack), whose new paintwork cannot disguise an old problem – the inherent weakness of the Bf 109's spindly undercarriage

BALKAN INTERLUDE

With plans for a seaborne assault on the coast of southern England permanently shelved, Hitler's thoughts had turned to the arch-enemy in the east. Preparations for the attack on the Soviet Union – the invasion was set for May 1941 – were almost complete when the Führer's attention was perforce diverted to the Balkans.

Mussolini's ill-considered invasion of Greece the previous October had quickly run into difficulties. By the spring of 1941, Hitler's Axis partner had been pushed back into Albania, and was in serious trouble. Furthermore, the population of neighbouring Yugoslavia had demonstrated its unwillingness to be drawn into the same Axis camp by rising in revolt against their pro-German leaders.

Hitler could not afford to have such unrest at his back as his troops marched into Russia. First, therefore, Yugoslavia and Greece would have to be subjugated. As time was of the essence – the Führer had allowed himself just five months to conquer the Soviet Union before autumn's mud made movement in the east well nigh impossible – the Balkan campaign was to be a *Blitzkrieg* in the truest sense of the word.

The arrival in Austria of *Stab*, II. and III./JG 54's 77 Bf 109Es represented just a fraction of the aerial might being assembled by *Luftflotte* 4 along the northern and eastern frontiers of Yugoslavia. It was from these directions that the two-pronged assault on the recalcitrant Balkan state would be launched.

From Graz-Thalerhof the *Geschwaderstab* and Dietrich Hrabak's II. *Gruppe*, with 5. and 6. *Staffeln*, were to support 2. *Armee's* drive southwards on Zagreb. Meanwhile, 4. *Staffel* was sent to reinforce III./JG 54, under Arnold Lignitz, which had left Parendorf, in Austria, and staged down to Arad, in Rumania. From here their task was to provide cover for the pincer movement aimed at the Yugoslav capital, Belgrade.

Operation *Marita* began at 0520 hrs on 6 April 1941. Like all previous *Blitzkrieg* campaigns it opened with the deliberate targeting of the

Men and machines of 8./JG 54 at Arad, in Rumania. Among the pilots pictured here are two future Knight's Cross winners. Heinz Lange (wearing sunglasses) would receive the award after being posted to JG 51. Hans-Joachim Heyer (in peaked cap, facing Lange) would be honoured posthumously after being killed in a dogfight near Leningrad in November 1942

enemy's air force. In Yugoslavia, however, Hitler had added an extra dimension. Angered at the disruption of his time-table by the Yugoslav civil uprising, he personally ordered punitive mass air raids on Belgrade. But, in general, the Luftwaffe would again experience the same sort of aerial opposition as had been encountered over Poland, Belgium and the Netherlands – limited in scale, heroic, and short-lived.

On the first day over Belgrade, III. *Gruppe* were credited with a trio of Yugoslav Air Force Bf 109s destroyed. That claimed by the *Staffelkapitän* of 9./JG 54, Oberleutnant Hans-Ekkehard Bob (now wearing the Knight's Cross, presented a month earlier at Le Mans) took his total to 20. The second fell to Leutnant Max-Hellmuth Ostermann (for his ninth), and the third was future *Experte* Oberleutnanr Gerhard Koall's first kill.

Yugoslav bombers struck back violently, and a pair of Blenheims attacked III./JG 54's base at Arad. Both were brought down, one by *Gruppenkommandeur* Hauptmann Lignitz for his first victory with the *Geschwader*. Apart from one III. *Gruppe* fighter badly damaged at Arad, the only other casualty suffered on the opening day of *Marita* was a machine of the *Geschwaderstab* lost in unknown circumstances some 22 miles (35 km) south of the Austrian border.

The following day it was the turn of Oberleutnant Hans Philipp's attached 4. *Staffel*, which claimed four enemy Bf 109s during a Stuka escort mission. Philipp's double raised his own score to 25. One of the other two was the 16th for Oberfeldwebel Max Stotz.

7 April also brought the first successes for II./JG 54's *Staffeln* in the north. 5./JG 54 intercepted a formation of Yugoslav Blenheims sent to bomb Luftwaffe airfields in Hungary and claimed six of the raiders shot down. Two went to Oberleutnant Hubert 'Hubs' Mütherich. As with Lignitz's Blenheim the day before, these were Mütherich's first kills since joining JG 54. His opening eight had been scored with I./JG 77 before he replaced the fallen Roloff von Aspern as *Kapitän* of 5. *Staffel* back in November.

Two of the other bombers destroyed were credited to future Oak Leaves recipient Leutnant Wolfgang Späte and to Leutnant Josef Pöhs. For 'Joschi' Pöhs, who (like 4. *Staffel's* Max Stotz) was ex-Austrian Air Force, and had been a member of I./JG 76 from the very beginning, this was his eighth victory of the war.

As far as can be ascertained, 6. *Staffel's* only success of the campaign was also achieved on 7 April. But the Yugoslav Hurricane destroyed on this date was noteworthy for providing the first for another future Oak Leaves winner and 100+ *Experte*, Leutnant Hans Beisswenger.

Three more claims would be made by III. *Gruppe* – a Hurricane for Leutnant Erwin Leykauf (his sixth kill) and an Ikarus IK-2 (an indigenous Yugoslav fighter) apiece for Oberleutnants Bob and Koall. But within 72 hours aerial resistance had effectively been broken. Henceforth, JG 54's fighters would be employed for the most part in the ground-attack role, mainly against locomotives in order to disrupt Yugoslav army movements.

On 10 April Zagreb was reached and an independent state of Croatia was proclaimed in the north. Forty-eight hours later the first German troops entered Belgrade. As in previous campaigns, the Luftwaffe's supporting fighters leapfrogged forward too. Dietrich Hrabak's *Staffeln* left Graz for Fünfkirchen (Pecs), in south-east Hungary. III./JG 54 transferred first from Arad to Data, closer to the Rumanian-Yugoslav border, and thence

Such was the speed of the transfer to the Balkans that little luxuries like fuel bowsers had to be left behind. Hans Philipp and Dietrich Hrabak (first and second right) are amused by the groundcrews' attempt to refuel Leutnant Steindl's machine by hand from a single drum. Note the Ju 87 Stuka in the background and, beyond it, the burnt-out skeleton of a Yugoslav biplane

Emils of II./JG 54 gathered at Belgrade-Zemun at the close of the campaign in Yugoslavia, ready to be handed over to JG 77

across the frontier to Pancevo, some 15 miles (24 km) north-east of Belgrade. A final move, to Byelyina, west of the Yugoslav capital, on 16 April almost ended in disaster.

An advance party, landing in four Ju 52s, came under heavy enemy fire. For the first (but not the last) time during the course of the war, the *Geschwader's* 'black men' – aircraft mechanics and other groundcrew, so called for the colour of the overalls they wore – had to grab their weapons to defend themselves and their airfield from enemy attack. Supported by their own ground-strafing fighters, Byelyina was finally secured, but only at the cost of several ground staff killed or wounded and one Bf 109 written off in a crash-landing.

The following day the Yugoslav Army surrendered unconditionally. Ironically, it was on this date that JG 54 suffered its sole pilot fatality of the campaign, when Leutnant Heinböckel of Lignitz's *Gruppenstab* crashed near Pancevo.

Their part in the Balkan operations at an end, II. and III./JG 54 were ordered to assemble at Belgrade's Zemun (Semlin) combined civil airport and military air base. There they were instructed to hand over their *Emils* to JG 77, which would carry the fight southwards down through Greece. On 3 May the personnel of JG 54 set off by road and rail for Stolp-Reitz, in Pomerania, where brand-new Bf 109Fs awaited them.

For the past eight months – throughout II. and III./JG 54's perambulations, from the Pas de Calais to Germany, back to France, and then down into Austria and the Balkans – Hauptmann Hubertus von Bonin's I. *Gruppe* had remained in situ as guardians of the North Sea coastal belt under the temporary command of JG 1.

It was not an arduous duty in terms of contact with the enemy. By far the greater foe was the unpredictability of the weather over the German Bight, especially in mid-winter. That, and the condition of some of the smaller, outlying fields on which individual *Schwärme* were deployed, led to a spate of forced-landings and other accidents. More than a dozen of I./JG 54's Bf 109Es were damaged during this period, and two were written off completely. Four pilots were injured, but only one was killed – Feldwebel Paul Poncet of 2. *Staffel* lost his life when his *Emil* crashed near Wesermünde on 31 March 1941.

Victories were few and far between. The most successful pilot was, perhaps, 3. *Staffel's* Oberleutnant Adolf Kinzinger, who had claimed

two Spitfires in October 1940 and added a third – reportedly a high-altitude PR variant – which he brought down off Texel on 12 January 1941. At least three Blenheims were credited to the *Gruppe* in April.

The bomber destroyed by Feldwebel Konrad Schönweiss of 1./JG 54 off the island of Amrum on the 11th was almost certainly the No 18 Sqn machine lost that day during an anti-shipping sweep. The victim of 3./JG 54's Leutnant Otto Vinzent is believed to have been a No 110 Sqn aircraft shot into the sea north of Texel, but some doubt surrounds the identity of that claimed by Oberleutnant Gerhard Ködderitzsch, the *Kapitän* of 1. *Staffel.*

By mid-May 1941, while II. and III. *Gruppen* were familiarising themselves on their new *Friedrichs* at Stolp-Reitz, close to the Baltic coast, I./JG 54 had also begun converting to Bf 109Fs at Jever. This led to an even higher accident rate. Over the course of the next four weeks five of the *Gruppe's* new aircraft were damaged and four completely destroyed. Four pilots were injured, the first being Gerhard Ködderitzsch on 15 May.

One of the other three was an unknown NCO of 2. *Staffel,* a certain Unteroffizier Otto Kittel, who came down on the island of Spiekeroog, north of Jever, on 31 May. Few would then have guessed that Kittel, small of stature and reticent by nature, would rise to become JG 54's highest scorer of all before his death in action in the closing months of the war.

In addition, two I. *Gruppe* pilots lost their lives in accidents involving the new *Friedrichs* – Unteroffizier Harry Krause at Jever on 4 June, and Fähnrich Arno Gäfke, who was killed in a mid-air collision with another Bf 109F over Langeoog four days later.

By contrast, II. and III./JG 54's conversion seems to have been accomplished relatively uneventfully. One pilot, 7. *Staffel's* Leutnant Max Clerico, was injured in an accident at Stolp-Reitz on 17 May, and exactly one month later, on 17 June, Gefreiter Liebgott of 9./JG 54 was lost when he came down in the sea off Stolpmünde.

Within 72 hours of this final accident JG 54 found itself once again re-united as a complete *Geschwader* – for only the second time since the outbreak of hostilities – on a cluster of forward landing grounds around Gumbinnen, close to East Prussia's outermost frontier with the former Baltic state of Lithuania (which had been incorporated as a Republic of the Soviet Union in August 1940).

JG 54 was about to embark upon the most successful period in its short but eventful history. Operation *Barbarossa*, the invasion of the Soviet Union, would bring with it victories in hitherto unimaginable numbers. Individual scores would no longer be measured in single figures, but in dozens – and, in some cases, in hundreds. The *Geschwader's* leading *Experten* would become national heroes, feted in the press and on the weekly newsreels. But the campaign which would deliver the 'Green Hearts' their greatest triumphs, would also prove to be their ultimate Nemesis.

On arrival at Stolp-Reitz little time was lost in giving II. *Gruppe's* brand new *Friedrichs* the same distinctive camouflage scheme as their predecessors

RUSSIA 1941-43

The opening salvoes of Operation *Barbarossa*, which shattered the pre-dawn darkness shortly after 0300 hrs on 22 June 1941, heralded the start of the greatest land invasion in the history of warfare. Over three million German troops began to advance across the borders of the Reich and into Soviet territory.

The 990-mile (1600 km) length of the main front was divided into three major axes of advance. In the south, *Heeresgruppe Süd* was to drive through the Ukraine to the shores of the Black Sea and beyond. In the centre, *Heeresgruppe Mitte* would strike across White Russia in the direction of Moscow. To the north, *Heeresgruppe Nord* was to advance through the three Soviet-occupied Baltic states of Lithuania, Latvia and Estonia towards Leningrad.

Major Hannes Trautloft's 105 serviceable Bf 109s (plus a further 33 of two temporarily attached *Staffeln* of JG 53) provided the sole fighter component of *Luftflotte* 1, the air command tasked with covering the northern sector thrust aimed at Leningrad.

Like all previous *Blitzkrieg* campaigns – albeit on a much larger scale – *Barbarossa* opened with targeted attacks on the enemy's air force. These achieved spectacular results (even the Luftwaffe's own High Command was at first reluctant to believe the reports from frontline units as to the numbers of Soviet aircraft destroyed). In the first 24 hours it was estimated that the Red Air Force had lost more than 1800 machines – over 300 to Luftwaffe fighters and flak, together with some 1500 destroyed on the ground!

Most of these latter casualties had been sustained on the central and southern sectors, where Soviet frontier airfields, packed with hundreds of aircraft 'lined up in serried ranks as if on parade', had been subjected to savage low-level bombing and ground-strafing attacks. In the north, JG 54's early operations consisted primarily of flying escort to Lfl. 1's three Ju 88-equipped *Kampfgeschwader* as they raided Russian airbases

Operation *Barbarossa* – a Bf 109F-2 of II./JG 54 gets a final check-over before the launch of the greatest land invasion in the history of warfare

Among those to claim victories on 22 June 1941, the opening day of *Barbarossa*, was I. *Gruppe's* Hauptmann Reinhard Seiler. The 'Top hat' beneath the cockpit sill of his *Friedrich* was a personal marking, a reminder of his days with 3. J/88 in Spain

some 60 miles (100 km) or more beyond the Lithuanian border. But here, too, successes were achieved.

On the opening day of the campaign Oberleutnant Adolf Kinzinger, *Staffelkapitän* of 1./JG 54, added a quartet of Soviet machines to his earlier western victories (Kinzinger would himself be lost over the coast of Lithuania five days later). 22 June also saw doubles for I. *Gruppe's* Hauptmann Reinhard Seiler and Leutnant Günther Raub – each of whom got a pair of Tupolev SB-2s, the latter's claimed in the space of 60 seconds – and a first for future Knight's Cross holder Unteroffizier Fritz Tegtmeier.

On the other side of the coin, 23 June was to witness JG 54's first casualties of the eastern front. Three pilots were reported killed, two in a mid-air collision, and a fourth missing. Fortunately, the latter (none other than Oberleutnant Hans-Ekkehard Bob, the *Kapitän* of 9. *Staffel*) was soon returned to his unit safe and sound.

Despite its enormous losses, the Soviet air force was quick to hit back. But its bomber forces were disorganised and expended in penny-packet numbers. As Hannes Trautloft noted in his diary at the time;

'The enemy air force is operated in a stubborn and uncoordinated manner, but it continues to fight, and occasionally delivers a nasty knock to our attacking spearheads.'

29 June was a day of just such raids, with wave after wave of Soviet bombers thrown against the River Düna bridges in a desperate attempt to stop the tanks of *Panzergruppe* 4 advancing into Latvia. But the day-long succession of attacks by enemy bombers, rarely in more than squadron strength and each rigidly holding to a predetermined course and nearly all devoid of fighter escort, gave the 'Green Hearts' their first major success of the Russian campaign.

By the time night fell – and with the vital bridges at Dünaburg still intact – the *Gruppe* had claimed no fewer than 65 Soviet bombers, including a brace of Ilyushin DB-3s for the *Kommodore* in one of the mid-afternoon raids, without loss.

Again in true *Blitzkrieg* fashion it was now time for JG 54's fighters to begin moving forward to keep pace with the advancing ground forces. On 30 June II. and III. *Gruppen* left Trakehnen and Blumenfeld, their jumping-off points in East Prussia, for Kowno (Kaunas), in Lithuania.

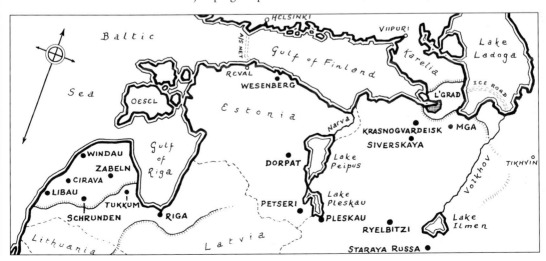

Illustrating the close co-operation between air and ground forces, Major Hannes Trautloft (left) confers with Generaloberst Busch, GOC 16. *Armee* (centre) and *General der Flieger* Förster, AOC I. *Fliegerkorps* (right), as the advance on Leningrad gathers pace. This photograph was taken at Dünaburg on 6 July 1941

Twenty-four hours later I./JG 54 leapfrogged past them, vacating Rautenberg/Lindental for two bases in Latvia – Mitau, some 25 miles (40 km) south-west of the Latvian capital Riga, and Birzi, near Jakobstadt on the west bank of the River Düna. It was on this same 1 July that Hauptmann Hubertus von Bonin relinquished command of I. *Gruppe* to Hauptmann Erich von Selle.

In the four days from 4 to 7 July the *Geschwader* added a further 109 Soviet aircraft to its collective scoreboard as it supported the continuing advance of the ground forces out of Latvia and into the Soviet Union proper. In the same period JG 54's casualties totalled just two killed (one in a light communications aircraft) and a third wounded.

By the end of the first week of July Lithuania and Latvia were entirely in German hands. Over the course of the next few days 'Green Heart' fighters would touch down for the first time on Russian soil as they began to occupy forward landing grounds south of Lakes Peipus and Pleskau (Pskov).

On 11 July I. *Gruppe* was the first to move in to Sarudinye. This small, primitive dirt strip was to be its home for nearly two months. Pilots and groundcrews alike lived under canvas, which did little to protect them against either the blazing heat of the summer sun or the clouds of choking dust which were thrown up every time an aircraft took off from the baked earth runway. Within weeks, Sarudinye had been enlarged (but not improved) to accommodate the whole *Geschwader* and, in August, the two other *Gruppen* were transferred in from similar fields in the nearby Ostrov and Lake Samra regions.

As the story goes, it was early on the morning of 11 July that III. *Gruppe's* Leutnant Waldemar Wübke was woken by the noise of his fighter's engine being test-run directly next to

That seemingly inseparable pair, Oberleutnant Hans Philipp (left) and Hauptmann Dietrich Hrabak (right) take a few seconds out for a quick drink and a bite during the near constant round of operations on the road to Leningrad

his tent. Still half asleep, and clad only in nightshirt and bedroom slippers, Wübke emerged from the tent for a wash and shave. His face covered in lather, he was suddenly aware that the sound of the Bf 109's engine being throttled back had been replaced by the barking of flak guns as two Soviet bombers streaked at low-level across the field.

'Hein' Wübke flip-flopped back to his fighter as fast as his slippered feet would carry him, yelling for its engine to be restarted. He took off and gave chase in the wake of the fleeing raiders. Catching up with them just before they reached friendly territory, he succeeded in shooting one down.

When he landed back at base, the onlookers' jubilation turned to merriment as he climbed out of the cockpit. His nightshirt had ridden right up under his chin. But as he explained to the admiring throng, 'An early morning flight like that in just a nightshirt is damned cold. From now on I'm wearing pyjamas!'

On 14 July, little more than three weeks after the start of *Barbarossa*, a strong, mixed-weapons battle group forced a crossing of the River Luga east of Lake Peipus. The Luga was the last natural frontier before Leningrad, which now lay only 65 miles (105 km) ahead of *Heeresgruppe Nord's* armoured spearheads.

Four days later JG 54 was to claim its 500th Soviet kill, which took its overall wartime score to more than 800. But 18 July also witnessed the loss of Leutnant Günther Raub, whose two SB-2s, brought down just before 0600 hrs on 22 June, had been among the first of the *Geschwader's* Russian victories.

While JG 54's three *Gruppen* had been supporting the main thrust of the ground advance – 16. *Armee's* direct overland drive across Lithuania and Latvia, past the southern tip of Lake Pleskau and then north-eastwards towards Leningrad – another *Staffel* had been following 18. *Armee's* more circuitous progress along the Baltic coastline with the aim of crossing the 30-mile (50 km) stretch of the Estonian-Soviet border between the northern shores of Lake Peipus and the sea.

As mentioned earlier, the *Geschwader's Ergänzungsstaffel* (which had been activated at Bergen, in Holland, back in October 1940, before commencing operations out of Katwijk) had been expanded into an *Ergänzungsgruppe* in February 1941. This *Gruppe*, based at Cazaux on the French Biscay coast, and commanded by Oberleutnant Eggers, consisted of just two *Staffeln* – 1.(*Einsatz*) and 2.(*Ausbildung*).

As their titles indicate, each of these *Staffeln* had a specific function. Trainees arriving fresh from fighter pilot school would first receive instructional (*Ausbildung*) training with 2. *Staffel*, before graduating to 1. *Staffel* for final operational (*Einsatz*) training prior to posting to one of the *Geschwader's* frontline units.

In the weeks leading up to *Barbarossa* the 70+ trainee pilots of ErgGr/JG 54 were transferred from France to Neukuhren, in East Prussia. From here the more advanced pupils of Oberleutnant Günther Fink's 1.(*Einsatz*) *Staffel* would receive first-hand operational experience as they accompanied 18. *Armee's* advance along the coastlines of the three Baltic states. Their bases along the way would include Windau (Ventspils), on the seaward side of Latvia's Kurland peninsula, the Latvian capital Riga itself, Pernau (Pärnu), on the coast of Estonia, and the latter's offshore island of Ösel (Saaremaa), which guarded the entrance to the Gulf of Riga.

Kommodore **Hannes Trautloft celebrates the *Geschwader's* 500th victory since the start of *Barbarossa*. Note for the first time the appearance of the 'Green Heart' of JG 54, complete with the badges of the unit's three component *Gruppen***

But these Baltic seaboard 'nursery slopes' were not altogether without danger, as a number of Günther Fink's pilots found to their cost. At least four would be killed before 1.(*Eins.*)/JG 54 crossed into Russia. And one 20-year-old Austrian leutnant by the name of Walter Nowotny narrowly escaped sharing their fate.

Nowotny's 24th operational mission, on 19 July, was to be as leader of a two-aircraft *Freie Jagd* over Ösel. Circling above the island's main Soviet airfield at Arensburg (Kuressaare), the pair watched as ten Russian fighters were scrambled. 'After a hairy dogfight, two of the Curtiss (sic) I-153s became my first two victories', Nowotny later wrote.

In the excitement Nowotny had lost his wingman. But with his fuel running low, there was little time to linger over Ösel. Reporting his position over the R/T, Nowotny set out alone to cross the 50-mile (80 km) stretch of the Gulf of Riga which separated him from his mainland base.

Almost immediately he spotted a white-nosed machine closing in behind him. Believing it to be his errant wingman (the *Staffel's* Bf 109E-7s wore white spinners), Nowotny waggled his wings in recognition. But as the 'wingman' drew nearer, its true identity was revealed. The *Emils* they flew were admittedly somewhat ancient, but they were definitely not biplanes! The aircraft sitting on his tail was hostile – as it promptly proceeded to demonstrate by pumping Nowotny's 'White 2' full of machine-gun bullets.

In his subsequent account, Nowotny describes his engine's holding out long enough for him to despatch his attacker (although his log-book entry mentions just his first two victims). But with his propeller at a standstill, he was soon looking for a suitable spot to make a forced-landing. Although still over the island, he discarded the option of belly-landing on firm ground, which would result in almost inevitable Soviet captivity. Instead, he chose to come down in the water close to a sandbank off the southern tip of Ösel. What followed drove him to the brink of suicide.

For three days he drifted in his tiny dinghy – at the mercy of the treacherous currents of the Irben Straits, on one occasion almost run down unnoticed by a Soviet destroyer – until finally being washed ashore on the Latvian coast.

But, quickly recovering from his ordeal, Nowotny was back in the air before the month was out. On 31 July he shot up a Beriev MBR-2 flying boat north-west of Ösel and claimed an Ilyushin DB-3 bomber south of the island – the very area where he himself had gone down – to begin a career which would take him into the ranks of the *Jagdwaffe's* true *élite*.

Meanwhile, on 27 July, Major Hannes Trautloft had been awarded the Knight's Cross for his 20th kill (a Tupolev SB-3 downed three days earlier). And on 31 July leading elements of 16. *Armee* reached the

Operational activity at II./JG 54's Lake Samra base was put on hold for a brief while on 6 August as the *Gruppe* celebrated the award of two more Knight's Crosses. One of a whole series of photographs commemorating the occasion, this shot shows Oberleutnant Hubert Mütherich (left) and Leutnant Josef Pöhs (right). Between them, flanking the rudder of Pöhs'(?) *Friedrich*, are Philipp and Hrabak

But there was another side to the coin. On that same 6 August Oberleutnant Reinhard Hein of 2. *Staffel* was brought down by enemy anti-aircraft fire close to the Baltic coast. Red Army soldiers examine his 'Black 1'. Hein would spend eight years in Soviet captivity before returning to Germany in 1949

The rapid advance along the coastal belt brought problems of its own. This pair of Bf 109Fs, seen on the recently occupied island of Oesel at the mouth of the Gulf of Riga, have outstrippd their supply train and are refuelling direct from an Me 321 transport glider specially flown in for the purpose. Although the nearest machine bears the markings of the *Geschwader* IA (operations officer), both are possibly 'hand-me-downs' that are now being operated by 1.(*Eins*)/JG 54

shores of Lake Ilmen, due south of Leningrad.

Twenty-four hours later Leutnant Max-Hellmuth Ostermann was credited with JG 54's 1000th victory of the war (although one source accords this honour to Oberleutnant Günther Scholz). That night, 1-2 August, Oberleutnant Georg Ruland was killed in a Soviet bombing raid on 3. *Staffel's* landing strip at Mal-Osvischi. Ruland was the first of seven pilots lost by JG 54 that month. Successes still far outnumbered casualties, however, and August saw a trio of decorations awarded.

On 6 August two members of 5./JG 54 received the Knight's Cross – *Staffelkapitän* Hubert Mütherich and Leutnant Josef Pöhs. At the beginning of the war the recognised norm for winning the Knight's Cross had been 20 enemy aircraft destroyed. But such were the numbers of Soviet machines now being shot down that this measure was already being increased. 'Hubs' Mütherich's and 'Joschi' Pöhs' individual scores reflect this. At the time of the award the former had 31 victories to his credit, and the latter 28.

As the war progressed, the number of kills required to attain this coveted decoration would rise even higher until, towards its close, there were pilots of JG 54 with more than 100 victories to their name but no Knight's Cross around their neck.

The situation regarding the next highest stage of the award, the Oak Leaves to the Knight's Cross – and those above – would develop along similar lines. Again, in the early months of the war the obligatory total to ensure the Oak Leaves was 40 enemy aircraft destroyed. But when Oberleutnant Hans Philipp, *Staffelkapitän* of 1./JG 54, was awarded the *Geschwader's* first Oak Leaves, on 24 August, his score had already reached 62.

By this time 18. *Armee* was advancing eastwards along the Gulf of Finland. With 16. *Armee's* offensive having smashed the Red Army's defences along the line of the River Luga, and now driving hard north-eastwards towards Leningrad – and with Germany's Finnish allies to the north of it – Soviet Russia's second city was in imminent danger of encirclement.

But the broiling summer sun of July was already a thing of the past, and the present weather conditions were not helping air operations, as Hannes Trautloft complained in his diary;

'It's a crying shame. Every day a few hours of sunshine, and then the north-westerlies bring thick clouds and heavy rain showers whipping in across our airstrips. The enemy's bombers and fighters manage to escape into them time and again. Every victory requires careful thought and a good deal of cunning. Each must be hard flown and hard fought for.'

But not always, apparently, as this less pessimistic extract illustrates:

'I can often follow the course of an engagement on the radio. The other day above the Luga bridges, for example, I heard the noise of Leutnant Pöhs – his lilting Austrian dialect unmistakable even over the R/T – asking, "Please, where are the *Ratas*?" He was answered in brusque East Prussian tones, "Nix *Ratas*, friendly fighters behind us!" That didn't go down well with a third party, who broke in heatedly, "Thanks a lot for 'friendly fighters' – these guys are already shooting at me!" which, in turn, must have confirmed the suspicions of a fourth, who cheerfully announced, "Aha! So they are Russians after all! Am attacking now!" That could only have been Philipp, Späte, Pöhs and Co.'

On 5 September – the day after Leutnant Max-Hellmuth Ostermann became the eighth member of the *Geschwader* to receive the Knight's Cross (for 29 victories) – JG 54 bade farewell to Sarudinye and moved forward to Siverskaya, an ex-Soviet airfield just under 40 miles (65 km) due south of Leningrad.

This base, together with Krasnogvardeisk (also known as Gatchina) some 15 miles (24 km) closer to the beleaguered city, would be home to the 'Green Hearts' for the best part of the next two years.

By the second week of September, air operations against Leningrad and the Soviet Baltic Fleet's main offshore base at Kronstadt were about to begin in earnest. The ring had now closed around the city. But it was not to be fought over and occupied. On 10 September Hitler had spelled out his

Once arrived on the Leningrad front, the pilots of I. Gruppe were in for something of a surprise. Their home for the coming months was to be in one wing of this imposing edifice, the one-time summer palace of the Russian czars, close to their Krasnogvardeisk base. Although they had to share the accommodation with *Luftflotte* 1's bomber and Stuka units, rarely can there have been a more majestic billet in the annals of aerial warfare!

By contrast, II and III./JG 54 had to 'slum it' in the far less palatial surroundings made available to them at Siverskaya. But here, too, there were compensations, including a camp cinema and home-built sauna

Siverskaya also housed the *Geschwader's* HQ, the entrance to which was guarded by a pair of stuffed bears. The larger of the two (the other was less than half its size) even towered above the tall figure of Hannes Trautloft, who is seen here (centre) welcoming *General der Jagdflieger* Adolf Galland during a visit in the summer of 1942. Note the 'Green Heart' on the boot of the staff car on the right

intentions. Leningrad, he decreed, was to be 'sealed off, bombarded, and starved out'. It was in pursuance of these aims stated from Berlin that most of the *Geschwader's* energies would be expended in the months ahead.

The campaign did not get off to a good start for JG 54. On 9 September they had lost their first Knight's Cross holder when Oberleutnant Hubert Mütherich, the *Kapitän* of 5. *Staffel*, was killed while attempting an emergency landing. 'Hubs' Mütherich's score was standing at 43 at the time of his death.

Forty-eight hours later 7./JG 54's Leutnant Peter Freiherr von Malapert-Neufville was shot down by MiG-3s near Lake Ilmen and taken prisoner. Impressed perhaps by their captive's aristocratic lineage, the Soviet propaganda machine quickly got to work. Within days leaflets bearing an appeal to surrender, purportedly signed by Peter von Malapert, fluttered down near Siverskaya.

By mid-September the *Geschwader's* pilots were each flying several missions a day. They provided escorts for the *Luftflotte's* bomber and Stuka units, which were not only bombarding Leningrad, but also supporting ground operations along the Volkhov front running south from the city to the shores of Lake Ilmen. They mounted *Freie Jagd* missions, and carried out low-level attacks behind enemy lines, once again targeting locomotives (shades of the Balkan campaign!) to disrupt the Soviet Army's rear area lines of supply.

For five days, between 21 and 25 September, they flew cover for Stukas dive-bombing the Soviet fleet in Kronstadt harbour (which resulted in the destruction of the 23,600-ton battleship *Marat* by a certain Oberleutnant Hans-Ulrich Rudel).

Despite this punishing operational schedule – at the height of which, on 18 September, 6. *Staffel's* Hauptmann Franz Eckerle was awarded the Knight's Cross for 30 confirmed kills – the 'Green Hearts' carried out

The last of the trio of JG 54's 'permanent' bases during the period of the Leningrad siege came a very poor third, if this aerial view from one of the *Geschwader's* Storch runabouts is anything to go by. In fact, Ryelbitzi was little more than a forward landing ground used for operations on the southernmost flank of *Luftflotte* 1's sector

But even Krasnogvardeisk had its drawbacks, as witness the sorry state of Oberleutnant Heinz Lange's 'White 1', peppered by shrapnel from Soviet long-range artillery bombardment

Hauptmann Arnold Lignitz, *Gruppenkommandeur* of III./JG 54, reportedly scored just five Soviet kills, bringing his overall total to 25, before he was lost over Leningrad on 30 September

their multifarious missions without loss. But the severity of the previous three months' hard campaigning was beginning to show in their serviceability figures which, by mid-September, had fallen to well below half the numbers they had deployed at the start of *Barbarossa*.

Still the only *Jagdgeschwader* assigned to the northern sector of the front (a position it would occupy for almost the entire remaining course of the war), JG 54's area of responsibility now stretched some 250 miles (400 km) from the Gulf of Finland in the north down to Demyansk beyond the southern tip of Lake Ilmen. Even with access to bases in the latter area, including Ryelbitzi and Staraya Russa (to the west and south of Lake Ilmen respectively), it was a huge length of front for the *Geschwader's* depleted strength to cover, and many missions were being flown in only *Schwarm* (four aircraft) or even *Rotte* (two aircraft) strength.

But it was Leningrad which remained its main focus of attention. And it was here that III./JG 54 lost their *Gruppenkommandeur* on the last day of September. Hauptmann Arnold Lignitz was engaged in a dogfight when a wing broke off his Bf 109F-2. Whether this was as a result of combat damage or structural failure is not clear. The early *Friedrichs'* propensity to shed a wing during violent manoeuvres was well known, and had already caused a number of fatalities, including Major Wilhelm Balthasar, *Geschwaderkommodore* of JG 2 'Richthofen' in the west.

Lignitz managed to extricate himself from his spinning machine and take to his parachute. He was observed drifting down over the centre of Leningrad, after which he disappeared without trace. It is presumed that he perished in one of the city's prisons.

Hauptmann Reinhard 'Seppl' Seiler was appointed *Kommandeur* of III. *Gruppe* on 1 October. Four days later 5./JG 54's Oberleutnant Wolfgang Späte – who would rise to become *Kommodore* of the Me 163-equipped JG 400 during the closing stages of the war – received the month's only Knight's Cross for his 45 victories to date.

October's operations would cost seven pilots reported killed or missing (although at least one of the latter pair, Unteroffizier Gerhard Proske, was to return to 1. *Staffel* ten days (!) after his forced-landing behind enemy lines). The *Geschwader's* activities, however, were increasingly governed by the worsening weather. Late August's unseasonably heavy showers had now given way to more persistent, and predictable, rain, which was turning unpaved landing strips and taxiways into lakes of mud.

By mid-October rapid movement was becoming impossible as the Soviet Union's primitive dirt roads were churned into quagmires by the unaccustomed weight of *Wehrmacht* traffic. It was the very situation Hitler had sought to avoid when he initially scheduled the launch of *Barbarossa* for May. The month's delay to this original timetable, brought about by the campaign in the Balkans, was to prove fateful.

But if conditions in October were bad, November was infinitely worse as the rain turned to snow, temperatures plummeted and the ground froze solid. On 8 November Hannes Trautloft, who had added five more Russian aircraft to his personal score during October, wrote in his diary;

'Despite the snow and cold, today's advance by the ground troops against Tikhvin progressing well, even without air cover. They have crossed the Tikhvin-Novaya Ladoga railway line, so the last rail connection to Leningrad is now in our hands.'

Tikhvin was some 100 miles (160 km) east of Leningrad. It was here that 8. *Staffel's* Leutnant Hans-Werner Paulisch had disappeared on 4 November (the 27th pilot lost since the start of *Barbarossa*) before the weather curtailed air operations. Although Trautloft's diary entry was correct, and the Tikhvin-Novaya Ladoga rail link had been severed, the

The first falls of snow herald the approach of 'General Winter'. A pair of 'black men' help guide a machine of 7./JG 54 out of its dispersal area . . .

. . . only to get a faceful of snow for their pains as the pilot guns his machine . . .

. . . once out on the runway each pilot carries out a final check while awaiting the order to take off

citizens of Leningrad still had one last life-line – the 7000 square mile (18,000 km) expanse of Lake Ladoga at their backs.

The precarious German toehold on the southernmost tip of the lake had, it is true, completed the land encirclement of the city. But from Novaya Ladoga, and other ports further around Ladoga's eastern shore, a trickle of supplies and reinforcements continued to be ferried into Leningrad – by small vessels during the summer months, and by road convoys across its frozen surface during the winter. Throughout the 900-day siege of Leningrad, attempts to disrupt this lake traffic would also figure prominently alongside JG 54's many other commitments.

But, in another respect, Trautloft's diary could not have been more wrong. The Tikhvin offensive was not 'progressing well'. It ground to a halt early in December as temperatures in the area dropped to 30 degrees below zero. On 8 December the High Command ordered an immediate cessation of all major offensive operations on the eastern front. German ground forces prepared to dig in for the winter.

But a Soviet counter-attack against the northern sector on 9 December forced *Heeresgruppe Nord* into its first retreat of the campaign as the XXXIX. *Panzerkorps* was pushed back from its forward positions around Tihkvin. In appalling conditions – the thermometer had suddenly plunged another 10 degrees – the surviving tanks and motorised infantry floundered through deep snow back across the Volkhov, the river line linking Lake Ladoga in the north to Lake Ilmen in the south.

The 'Green Hearts' played little part in these proceedings. Like the rest of the *Wehrmacht*, they had been taken completely by surprise by the severity and suddenness of the Russian winter, and had not yet learned the local 'tricks of the trade' which enabled the Red Air Force to keep flying under the most adverse of conditions. After 1. *Staffel's* Unteroffizier Erwin Löffler was reported missing on 3 December, the remainder of the month's losses were material, with a dozen *Friedrichs* being damaged or written-off on the ground – mainly at Siverskaya and Krasnogvardeisk, and either due to enemy raids (as indicated by Trautloft's diary) or as the result of accidents.

On 20 December Hauptmann Reinhard Seiler, *Gruppenkommandeur* of III./JG 54, was awarded the *Geschwader's* eighth and last Knight's Cross of the year (for 42 victories). On the same day Hauptmann Erich von Selle relinquished command of I. *Gruppe* to Hauptmann Franz Eckerle, erstwhile *Staffelkapitän* of 6./JG 54. December also saw II. *Gruppe's* withdrawal to Uetersen, in northern Germany, for rest and re-equipment with Bf 109F-4s.

On 31 December 1941, 1. *Staffel's* Unteroffizier Karl Schnörrer, who had joined the *Geschwader* some six months earlier, claimed his first kill. Nicknamed 'Quax' (something of a back-handed compliment, being derived from a popular film of the period chronicling the adventures of an accident-prone pilot), Schnörrer himself was, by eastern front

Despite the rapidly worsening conditions, sorties continued to be flown from dawn till dusk. The adjutant of III. *Gruppe* **eases himself into his cockpit in the grey light of early morning. His** *Friedrich* **has been given a very rudimentary coat of white winter camouflage over the wing and tailplane uppersurfaces and along the dorsal spine . . .**

standards, not a high scorer. But he later became an integral part of a formidable team when flying as long-term wingman to Walter Nowotny.

In 1941 *Heeresgruppe Nord* had been able to carry out a series of spectacular advances from the Lithuanian border to the gates of Leningrad and beyond. But for the German air and ground units engaged in the north, the new year was to bring with it campaigning of a very different kind.

For while operations on the Russian front in 1942 were to be dominated by events in the far south – the hugely ambitious, but ultimately catastrophic, two-pronged offensive aimed at capturing the twin prizes of the Caucasian oilfields and the city of Stalingrad – the war in the northern sector would degenerate into a near static slugging match.

... whereas, although difficult to see against the setting sun, this machine of III./JG 54 returning at the end of the day has a more elaborate green and white segmented camouflage scheme. Even harder to make out is the bent aerial mast and sagging antenna. The cause of this minor damage is not known

Although no less ferocious than the wide-ranging tank battles fought over the open expanse of steppe to the south, territorial gains in the north would be measured not in hundreds of miles, but in tens, as each side sought to dislodge the other from its established positions.

By January 1942 these positions had solidified along the 100 miles (160 km) or so of the Volkhov front from Lake Ladoga down to Lake Ilmen, and thence approximately another 80 miles (130 km) south-eastwards to Lake Selig, which marked the boundary with *Heeresgruppe Mitte*. It was along these two stretches – together with its continuing commitments over Leningrad – that much of JG 54's war would be fought in the months ahead.

Hauptmann Franz Eckerle, I. *Gruppe's* new *Kommandeur*, celebrated New Year's Day by claiming a trio of Soviet fighters – a pair of I-16s during the morning's mission from Krasnogvardeisk and a solitary I-153 in the early afternoon. But 1942 began on a far less happy note for III./JG 54 at Siverskaya, which was the target of a heavy bombing raid on the night of 2 January.

Once again displaying their ability to operate under the most extreme conditions (the temperature was now 45 degrees below zero!), the attackers inflicted considerable damage. One source quotes ten of the *Gruppe's* aircraft destroyed, while another lists five of its F-2s and ten light communications machines destroyed or damaged beyond repair. Fortunately, casualties among ground personnel were minimal, with one man killed and another four wounded.

In the second week of January the Soviets launched three separate counter-offensives – against the Volkhov front, where they smashed a breach 18 miles (30 km) wide in the German defences, against Staraya Russa, and against Ostashkov on the southern edge of Lake Selig, the army group's boundary with the central sector.

Luftflotte 1 directed its entire strength to the support of the embattled ground forces, and JG 54 was heavily committed over the most critical areas of the front. Hauptmann Hrabak's II. *Gruppe* was hastily recalled from Germany, flying its new F-4s into Dno, an airfield some 50 miles

(80 km) west of Staraya Russa. By the end of the month the *Geschwader* had been credited with 99 enemy aircraft shot down for the loss of just three pilots – I. *Gruppe's* Gefreiter Gustav Haubner was killed, and Leutnant Bruno Bluhm and Feldwebel Wilhelm Quak were both reported missing.

Among the many successful pilots was future Knight's Cross recipient Unteroffizier Rudolf Rademacher. Having joined 3. *Staffel* only three weeks earlier, Rademacher had claimed his first kill on 9 January. Like 'Quax' Schnörrer, he would later be a member of the famous Nowotny *Schwarm*.

Soon the snow was so deep that dispersals and taxiways had to be shovelled clear

During the latter half of January the attack across the Volkhov by the Soviet 2nd Assault Army had penetrated the German positions to a depth of 36 miles (58 km). This posed a potential threat to the ring around Leningrad, and forced the defenders to make 'all sorts of improvisations'. On the ground this meant, for example, employing rear-area supply troops in the line alongside combat units. And a new dimension was also introduced to the war in the air by the now Oberstleutnant Hannes Trautloft.

Deciding that the Red Air Force had had the night skies to itself for far too long (a view heartily endorsed by every German soldier who had been subjected to Soviet nocturnal bombing and harassment raids), Trautloft began experimenting by sending selected pilots up on bright moonlit nights to circle at low-level in areas of known intruder activity.

The experiment was an unqualified success. During the course of the Volkhov fighting, which lasted from mid-January to July 1942, Trautloft's 'nightfighters' – the first to operate on the eastern front – claimed 56 kills without loss.

The most successful exponent was III. *Gruppe's* 'Seppl' Seiler, who added 16 nocturnal kills to his overall score. Next came Oberleutnant Günther Fink, until recently an instructor with the *Ergänzungsgruppe*, who achieved nine. And third was Leutnant Erwin Leykauf, whose eight included six enemy supply aeroplanes brought down in the space of just one hour on the night of 22-23 June alone! This latter feat boosted Leykauf's total to 23, and won him an *Ehrenpokal* (honour cup), presented by Generaloberst Keller, the GOC of *Luftflotte* 1, for his 'outstanding achievements'.

On 4 February Oberfeldwebel Karl Kempf of III. *Gruppe* was awarded the first of JG 54's 12 Knight's Crosses of 1942 (for 41 kills, all by daylight).

By now it was the situation south of Lake Ilmen which was giving cause for concern. Soviet forces had

As winter tightened its grip, JG 54's aircraft were painted white overall to blend in with the near featureless, snow-covered landscape. Even the *Geschwader's* hacks, such as the Fw 58 at left, wore winter white as they went about their daily chores

Increased Red Army pressure early in 1942 called for an all-out effort by the Luftwaffe. Here, groundcrew from 6. *Staffel* prepare two of their charges – whose camouflage indicates a lot of wear and tear already – for yet another Ju 87 escort mission. The Stukas' 500-kg (1100-lb) bombs lie ready in the foreground

With an improvement in the weather longer range sorties were also flown as *Luftflotte* 1's bombers began to attack the Soviets' rear-area lines of supply. High above one of the northern sector's many lakes, 7. *Staffel's* 'White 6', whose rudder displays a modest eight victories, sits tight on the starboard wing of an He 111

continued to push westwards, bypassing and cutting off two German positions, which Hitler promptly designated 'strongholds'. Rather than allow them to fight their way out of encirclement, the 3500 defenders of Kholm and the 95,000 troops trapped in the much larger pocket at Demyansk were to be supplied by air until they could be freed by a counter-offensive. This would take the best part of three months, during which time protection of the transports flying the supply runs was added to JG 54's growing list of commitments.

Rather than attempt to provide close-escort for the slow and lumbering Ju 52 formations (which usually flew in groups of 20 to 40 machines), the 'Green Hearts' mounted *Freie Jagd* sweeps in *Schwarm* or *Rotte* strength along the approach and return routes to the two pockets, as well as over the drop zones and landing areas themselves. These tactics obviously paid off. By the end of February the *Geschwader* had added another 201 victories to its collective score, plus a further 359 during March.

But its own losses were also beginning to rise, slowly but perceptibly. On 14 February Hauptmann Franz Eckerle, *Kommandeur* of I. *Gruppe*, was brought down by ground fire south-west of Kholm. Since heading the first *Jabostaffel* on the Channel front in the latter stages of the Battle of Britain, Eckerle's total of confirmed aerial victories had risen to 59. On 12 March he would become the first member of JG 54 to be honoured posthumously with the Oak Leaves.

Nine days after Eckerle was posted missing, the *Geschwader* lost another of its long-serving pilots when Hauptmann Hans Schmoller-Haldy, who had been *Staffelkapitän* of 3./JG 54 since its inception, was seriously wounded. After a lengthy period of recovery, he joined the staff of the *General der Jagdflieger*, where he would remain until the end of the war.

The officer selected to replace Eckerle as I. *Gruppe's Kommandeur* was Hauptmann Hans Philipp, the *Staffelkapitän* of 4./JG 54. The new incumbent was soon proving his worth. Among Philipp's string of victories during the latter half of February were a pair of Curtiss P-40 Tomahawks (presumably of the 154th Regiment, one of the first Soviet units to operate the recently-delivered US type on the Leningrad front).

On 9 March the *Ergänzungsgruppe*, whose *Einsatzstaffel* was sharing Krasnogvardeisk with Philipp's I./JG 54, was officially disbanded. During their unit's 16-month history the *Geschwader's* trainee pilots had been credited with no fewer than 51 kills (the majority being claimed by the *Einsatzstaffel*).

Oberleutnant Max-Hellmuth Ostermann, *Staffelkapitän* **of 8./JG 54 (note the metal command pennant on the aerial mast of his 'Black 1'), was awarded the Oak Leaves on 10 March 1942 for 62 kills**

Even more successful, Hauptmann Hans Philipp, recently appointed *Kommandeur* **of I.** *Gruppe,* **became the first member of JG 54 to achieve the century. Caught at an unguarded moment, 'Fips' Philipp appears less than euphoric as he is photographed in front of a garland of pine branches at Krasnogvardeisk on 31 March 1942**

A new system of operational training was in turn put in place with the activation of an autonomous *Ergänzungsjagdgeschwader*, initially comprising two *Gruppen* – 'East' and 'West'. These latter designations were purely geographical, the eastern components being based at Liegnitz, Rogau-Rosenau and Sagan, in Lower Silesia, and the western at Bergerac, Biarritz and Toulouse, in occupied France.

Some semblance of the old order was retained, however, as the two ErgJGrs – 'East' and 'West' – were each composed of *Staffeln* which still trained pilots for specific operational units. JG 54 had a foot in both camps, its replenishments subsequently coming from its own *Erg. Staffeln* in either France or Germany. The new system also called for every *Jagdgeschwader* to provide experienced combat pilots to serve as instructors.

A number of JG 54's later Knight's Cross recipients – the likes of Anton Döbele, Otto Kittel, Hans-Joachim Kroschinski, Rudolf Rademacher and Wilhelm Schilling – all spent some time with one or other of the two *Ergänzungsstaffeln* readying young pilots for the rigours of frontline service.

The second week of March brought further honours for JG 54's two leading scorers. On the 10th Oberleutnant Max-Hellmuth Ostermann, now the *Kapitän* of 7. *Staffel*, was awarded the Oak Leaves for 62 victories. Forty-eight hours later Hauptmann Hans Philipp, with his total standing at 82, became the first member of the 'Green Hearts' to win the Swords.

By this time the situation along the Volkhov front south of Leningrad had been somewhat stabilised (a German pincer movement had cut off the advancing Soviet 2nd Assault Army and it was now the Russians who were encircled), and a narrow land corridor had been established to the Demyansk 'cauldron' south of Lake Ilmen.

Luftflotte 1 could now redirect part of its attention back to Leningrad itself or, more precisely, to the ships of the Soviet Baltic Red Banner Fleet in Kronstadt harbour, against whose heavy guns German troops on the nearby mainland had no defence. Beginning in late March, the fighters of JG 54 escorted the bombers and Stukas of I. *Fliegerkorps* in a series of concentrated attacks on the Russian vessels.

On 31 March the redoubtable 'Fips' Philipp made his mark yet again by becoming the first pilot of JG 54 (and only the fourth in the entire *Jagdwaffe*) to reach his century. And four days later 8. *Staffel's* Oberfeld-webel Rudolf Klemm was credited with the *Geschwader's* 2000th confirmed kill of the war.

The Führer's War Directive No 41, dated 5 April 1942, clearly shows that Hitler had undergone a change of mind regarding the fate of Leningrad. In it he states that '. . . *Heeresgruppe Nord* will capture Leningrad and link up with the Finns (on the Karelian Isthmus)'. This was only to take place, however, *after* the successful conclusion of the campaign in the south.

And although ground reinforcements were moved into the area, and a special command staff was set up at Siverskaya to oversee forthcoming air operations, the dramatic failure of the southern offensive – and a resurgence of Soviet activity along the Volkhov – meant that plans to recapture Leningrad were first put on hold, and then postponed indefinitely. The city had thus been spared the fate of Stalingrad, but – arguably even more gruelling – had been sentenced instead to a further 22 months under siege.

The cessation of the air attacks on the Soviet fleet at the end of April was a portent of things to come. Considerable damage had been inflicted on at least one battleship, two heavy cruisers and a number of smaller vessels. But the fleet's firepower had not been totally neutralised. And now *I. Fliegerkorps* was needed elsewhere on the front.

JG 54 continued its steady attrition of Soviet aircraft along the northern sector. During April the *Geschwader* had added another 261 victories to its overall total. 5. *Staffel's* Oberleutnant Wolfgang Späte was enjoying a particular run of success, including a pair of Pe-2s claimed on the morning of 16 April. Exactly a week later, with his score risen to 72, he was awarded the Oak Leaves.

Early in May the pockets at Kholm and Denyansk were finally freed. But although the Soviet Army had been pushed back, the growing strength of the Red Air Force kept the 'Green Hearts' fully occupied. The increased tempo of operations during the coming months was reflected in the lengthening victory lists, both collective and individual.

On 9 May two new names were added to the ranks of the *Geschwader's* Knight's Cross winners. Leutnants Hans Beisswenger and Horst Hannig, both of 6. *Staffel*, received their awards – for 47 and 48 kills respectively – from the hands of General Hellmuth Förster (GOC *I. Fliegerkorps*) during a brief ceremony at Ryelbitzi. But it was soon back to business as usual. That very afternoon a Soviet raid would net the *Kommodore* two more victories – a Yak-1 fighter and a twin-engined Pe-2.

Three days later Max-Hellmuth Ostermann, whose diminutive stature belied his ferocity in the air, became the second JG 54 pilot to achieve his century. Although himself severely wounded in the right arm and thigh during the dogfight over the Volkhov, the semi-conscious

There were certainly smiles in evidence at Ryelbitzi on 9 May when the *Geschwader* celebrated the award of two more Knight's Crosses. These individuals are, from left to right, Major Trautloft, Leutnant Hans Beisswenger, *General der Flieger* Förster, Leutnant Horst Hannig and Hauptmann Dietrich Hrabak

Displaying the solicitude for his men for which he was justly famous, Hannes Trautloft visits the wounded Max-Hellmuth Ostermann in the sick-bay at Siverskaya. Before his release from hospital Oberleutnant Ostermann would be awarded the Swords for his century

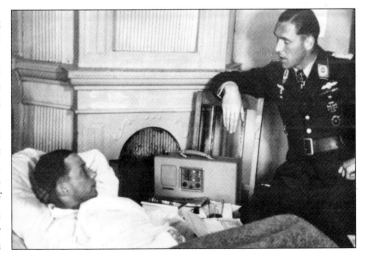

Ostermann managed to land his 'Black 1' safely back at Lyuban, one of the *Geschwader's* forward strips midway between Leningrad and Lake Ilmen. On 17 May, while still in hospital, Oberleutnant Ostermann was awarded the Swords.

Pressure continued throughout June, the month which was to see II. *Gruppe's* Oberfeldwebel Max Stotz – a member of the Austrian air arm's pre-war aerobatics team – receive the Knight's Cross (for 53 kills) on the 19th. Ten days later the River Volkhov battles finally ended with the annihilation of the Soviet break-through force.

During the first six months of 1942 pilots of JG 54 flew the eastern front's first unofficial nightfighter sorties, patrolling at low altitude on bright moonlit nights to catch Soviet intruders and transports dropping supplies to partisans behind German lines. Leutnant Erwin Leykauf claimed six of the latter in just one hour on the night of 22-23 June! Note his personal emblem (see page 77 for details) on the nose of his fighter

Among the many prisoners taken was the Commander of the 2nd Assault Army, Gen Andrei Vlasov, who would later form and lead the 'Russian Liberation Army' on the side of the Germans.

Until now JG 54's area of operations had been 'confined' to the fronts running south from Leningrad. But in June the *Geschwader* extended its presence northwards. The spring thaw had naturally brought a halt to the supplies reaching Leningrad via the 'ice road' across the frozen Lake Ladoga. By the early summer this lifeline had been replaced by ships, either singly or in small convoys, sailing from Novaya Ladoga and other harbours on the Soviet-held eastern side of the lake.

In an attempt to put a stop to this traffic, a small ad hoc naval force – four German coastal minelayers, four Italian navy torpedo-boats and about twenty Luftwaffe-manned Siebel ferries (landing vessels employed as floating gun platforms) – was established on the lake. And it would be JG 54's task to help protect it.

On 23 June a *Rotte* of 7. *Staffel* aircraft flew to Utti, in Finland, reportedly to finalise arrangements for the deployment. But it was not until early in July that the main force arrived. This comprised 15 F-4s drawn from 1. and 2./JG 54, which were based at Mensuvaara, on the north-western edge of Lake Ladoga, and at Petäjärvi. Headed by 2. *Staffel's* Oberleutnant Hans Götz, the *Kommando* would remain in Finland until early October 1942, when the onset of winter presaged the resumption of road traffic across the ice.

The *Rotte* of 7. *Staffel* Bf 109F-4s was sent to Utti on 23 June 1942 to finalise details of the *Kommando* to be based in Finland for the protection of the Axis naval flotilla on Lake Ladoga. In the foreground, with 20 kill bars on its rudder, is the *Friedrich* of *Staffelkapitän* Oberleutnant Friedrich Rupp

Kommandoführer **Oberleutnant Hans Götz of 2./JG 54 (right), who would lead the Lake Ladoga protection force, is seen in conversation with his Finnish counterpart, 56-kill ace Capt Eino Luukkanen of 1/LLv 24**

During this period the rest of the *Geschwader* enjoyed mixed fortunes along the other sections of the front, as ever increasing individual scores, and their concomitant awards, were offset by a lengthening list of losses – all keenly felt, but some more grievous than others. In July JG 54 had begun re-equipping with Bf 109G-2s. It was in one of the new *Gustavs* that Oberleutnant Ostermann, fully recovered from his wounds of mid-May, and now wearing the Swords, took off with his wingman, Unteroffizier Heinrich Bosin, on 9 August for a deep-penetration *Freie Jagd*.

Flying at an altitude of 3250 ft (1000 m) far behind Russian lines east of Lake Ilmen, the pair sighted nine Curtiss P-40s. Ostermann dived to the attack, opening fire on the rear machine from a range of just 30 yards (27 m). As large pieces broke off its starboard wing the two *Gustavs* zoomed up and away. They were just preparing to make a second pass when they themselves were bounced from behind by another group of Soviet fighters emerging from the broken cloud. A burst of fire hit Ostermann's cockpit. The canopy flew off and a bright tongue of flame erupted along the rear fuselage. The *Gustav* rolled over on to its port wing and dived into the ground at the edge of a small wood.

Twenty-four hours later the *Geschwader* lost another *Staffelkapitän* when 6./JG 54's Hauptmann Carl Sattig was reported missing near Rzhev, on the central sector – a Soviet offensive aimed at driving a wedge between the army group boundaries south of Lake Selig had resulted in II. *Gruppe's* temporary deployment to this area a few days earlier. Sattig, who had been a long-range reconnaissance pilot before joining JG 54 in 1941, would be awarded a posthumous Knight's Cross (for his 53 victories with the *Geschwader*) on 19 September.

Sattig and Ostermann's posts as *Kapitäne* of 6. and 8 *Staffeln* were filled by Leutnants Hans Beisswenger and Günther Fink respectively. On 21 August the 64 victories credited to Hauptmann Joachim Wandel, *Staffelkapitän* of 5./JG 54, won him the month's only Knight's Cross. 'Gnom' Wandel's operational career had begun with the *Legion Condor* in

In the summer of 1942 JG 54 began to receive its first Bf 109Gs. This is the *Gustav* of *Kommodore* Hannes Trautloft (see colour profile 17)

Wearing a brown and green camouflage scheme similar to Trautloft's machine, these G-2s bear the markings of II. (left) and III. *Gruppe* (right)

Apparently finished in dark greens overall, 9. *Staffel's* 'Black 1' has come to grief at Ryelbitzi. Minutes earlier its pilot, Leutnant Walter Nowotny, having downed three enemy aircraft during the course of the sortie, carried out three victory passes over the field despite his own machine having been damaged by cannon fire behind the cockpit and in the fuselage fuel tank. As this photograph shows, the high-scoring Nowotny ended the sortie in chequered style by performing a spectacular somersault on landing!

Spain, where he had been shot down by light anti-aircraft fire and spent some time in Republican captivity. Since then he had served both as *Kapitän* of 2./JG 76 and as the Adjutant of II. *Gruppe* under Dietrich Hrabak.

On 27 August the Red Army launched another heavy assault against the Volkhov front in a renewed attempt to relieve Leningrad, and once again it came to grief. After more than a month of heavy fighting, the last seven divisions (of the sixteen which had begun the attack) were encircled in the heavily forested area around Mga and forced to surrender on 2 October.

By this time a new and rapidly rising young star was making his presence felt in the air. Upon the dissolution of the *Ergänzungsgruppe* back in March those trainee pilots considered ready for frontline duty had been distributed among the operational *Staffeln*. One of their number was Walter Nowotny, who had survived three days adrift in a rubber dinghy, and who was now posted to Oberleutnant Koall's 3./JG 54.

A succession of victories – including seven on 2 August – had since raised Nowotny's total to 56, for which he finally received the Knight's Cross on 4 September. In a letter to his parents, dated 3 August, the young ace had already written that the previous day's seven kills should qualify him for the 'Tin Collar'!

On 14 September III. *Gruppe's* Leutnant Hans-Joachim Heyer scored the kills which gave the 'Green Hearts' their 3000th victory of the war. And before the month was out JG 54 had another 'centurion'. 'Beisser' ('Biter') Beisswenger claimed his hundredth on 26 September, an achievement duly acknowledged by the award of the Oak Leaves four days later.

As September drew to a close the main focus of land activity once again shifted southwards towards the area of Demyansk. The change of emphasis in ground operations had little material effect on the *Geschwader's* 90-odd serviceable *Gustavs* in the skies above, however, as they continued to pit themselves against the growing strength and confidence of the Red Air Force. The weeks ahead would bring the usual mix of successes counter-weighted by losses – that, and the inevitable prospect of yet another bitterly cold Russian winter.

On 6 October the 'Green Hearts' lost one of their true characters when Unteroffizier Anton 'Toni' Pfeifer – the world's reigning downhill ski champion – was killed in a dogfight south-east of Lake Ilmen. Twenty-four hours later Hauptmann Joachim Wandel suffered the same fate, in the same area, after downing a LaGG-3 for his 75th, and final, victory. 'Gnom' Wandel's 5. *Staffel* was led for a month by acting *Kapitän* Leutnant Horst Hannig before Oberleutnant Steindl was appointed to its head on 11 November.

The autumn rains presage the approach of a second Russian winter. 5. *Staffel's* 'Yellow 2' carefully skirts a large puddle

Other changes in command had by then taken place, but not before 9. *Staffel's* Wilhelm Schilling had been awarded October's one Knight's Cross. Schilling had been badly wounded by anti-aircraft fire after bringing down a heavily-armoured Il-2 on 16 September. The *Sturmovik* was Schilling's 46th victory. He was still in his hospital bed at Siverskay when *Staffelkapitän* Hans-Ekkehard Bob presented him with the decoration on 10 October.

On 25 October Oberleutnant Heinz Lange, who had been *Kapitän* of 1./JG 54 for just over a year, was posted to take command of 3./JG 51 on the neighbouring central sector. His replacement at the head of 1. *Staffel* was the up-and-coming Leutnant Walter Nowotny.

Two days after Lange's departure II./JG 54 lost its even longer serving *Kommandeur* when Major Dietrich Hrabak, who had been with the *Gruppe* since its formation as I./JG 76 in 1938, was appointed *Geschwaderkommodore* of JG 52 in the far south. The officer who arrived – albeit not until 19 November – to assume command of II./JG 54 was a stranger to the eastern front – Channel coast *Experte*, and Oak Leaves wearer, Hauptmann Hans 'Assi' Hahn who, for the last two years, had been *Kommandeur* of III./JG 2 'Richthofen'.

Maj Dietrich Hrabak (right) left the 'Green Hearts' in October 1942 to take command of JG 52 on the southern sector

Although the 'Green Hearts' were much better prepared, and equipped, to face their second eastern front winter, the deteriorating weather did slow the pace of operations to some extent. But there were those who actually seemed to thrive despite the elements. One such was II. *Gruppe's* leading NCO pilot, Oberfeldwebel Max Stotz, who reached his century on 29 October (for which he received the Oak Leaves the following day). It had taken Stotz some four-and-a-half months to raise his total from 50 to 100. It would take him less than three – in increasingly arctic conditions – to score his next fifty.

November's two Knight's Crosses were both posthumous – and both conferred upon pilots who had been lost over Leningrad. Feldwebel Peter Siegler of 3. *Staffel* had been killed over the city's dock area back on 24 September. His 48 victories resulted in the award of the Knight's Cross on 3 November. The second recipient was a more recent casualty. 8./JG 54's Leutnant Hans-Joachim Heyer was posted missing after a mid-air collision with a Soviet fighter on 9 November. His award was made 16 days later. Among Heyer's final score of 53 were six claimed by night while flying as one of Hannes Trautloft's experimental *Nachtjäger*.

Hrabak's successor at the head of II. *Gruppe* was Major Hans Hahn, a Channel front *Experte* who had scored 68 victories with JG 2 'Richthofen'. By 26 January 1943 he had added 32 Soviet kills to that figure to reach his century. Pictured at that evening's celebrations in the officer's mess in the village of Ryelbitzi, Major Hahn (left) is seen with Leutnant Max Stotz who, that very same day, had achieved 150 and Oberleutnant Hans Beisswenger (right), whose current tally was 131. Two points of interest – Adolf Galland's portrait at top right, and the fact that 'Assi' Hahn still wears the *Jagdgeschwader* Richthofen cuff title on his right sleeve

The shape of things to come – pilots of JG 54 are introduced to the Fw 190. Note the 'Green Heart' on the cowling and, somewhat mystifyingly, the III. *Gruppe* vertical bar on the rear fuselage – perhaps a machine on loan from JG 51 for purposes of familiarisation?

The last of 1942's 11 Knight's Crosses was won in happier circumstances when Oberleutnant Hans Götz of 2. *Staffel* was presented with the award on 23 December for his 48 confirmed kills.

The year, which had seen the *Geschwader* in almost constant action in defence of the northern sector, ended for the 'Green Hearts' in a fierce series of clashes with the enemy over the Demyansk-Staraya Russa areas, south of Lake Ilmen, on 30 December. Although three NCO pilots were lost in the day's actions, four of JG 54's highest scoring and most highly decorated pilots were able to add significantly to their personal totals.

Oberleutnant Beisswenger's four took his score to 119, while Hauptmann 'Assi' Hahn went one better with five. This raised his tally since arriving on the eastern front six weeks earlier to ten, and elevated his overall total to 78. Hauptmann Philipp claimed eight and thereby reached 130. But the now commissioned Leutnant Max Stotz outdid them all. He was credited with no fewer than ten enemy aircraft destroyed on this date. This jumped his score to 129 – well on the way to that next half-century, which he would attain on 26 January.

If the start of 1942 had transformed the tenor of JG 54's operations – with 1941's rapid advances through the Baltic states giving way to a more defensive posture over the Volkhov and Demyansk fronts – then the end of the year heralded even more fundamental changes, which would set the pattern for the final 30 months of the *Geschwader's* history. For the opening weeks of 1943 were to witness re-equipment with a new fighter, the arrival of new names and faces, the 'loss' of one complete *Gruppe* and, subsequently, the activation of another.

More significantly, perhaps, the ever growing strength of the enemy resulted in a new role for JG 54 as an aerial 'fire brigade', with components suddenly being despatched, for short or longer-term deployment, to whichever part of the front was then under the greatest threat. As Soviet pressure grew, fighters bearing the distinctive 'Green Heart' symbol would be seen along the whole length of the eastern front, from Finland in the north to the Crimea in the south.

On 6 January 1943 the *Geschwader's* two front runners, Hans Philipp and Max Stotz, claimed three and four kills respectively, which tied their scores at 133 apiece. Six days later the Red Army launched yet another offensive against the Volkhov front in an attempt to lift the siege of Leningrad. On that opening day 'Fips' Philipp downed seven enemy machines to bring his total to 146. Then, on 14 January, I./JG 54 was credited with 30 victories. Two of them had fallen to the *Gruppenkommandeur*, which, with a pair in the interim, meant that Philipp had become the first of the 'Green Hearts' to achieve 150.

January's two Knight's Crosses, however, went to the other *Gruppen*. On 22nd Oberfeldwebel Eugen-Ludwig Zweigart of 5./JG 54 gained his for 54 confirmed kills. Forty-eight

hours later ex-reconnaissance pilot Leutnant Friedrich Rupp of 7. *Staffel* was similarly decorated for 50 victories. It was two days later still that, on 26 January, Max Stotz got his 150th. This latter date also saw Hans Beisswenger take his total to 131, and Hans 'Assi' Hahn reach his century.

The first Focke-Wulfs arrived at Krasnogvardeisk in January 1943. As an Fw 190 disports overhead, a rather weary looking *Gustav* runs up its engine ready for the next sortie

While the high flyers (both figuratively and literally!) were scything into the Red Air Force formations above, another equally ferocious and no less important war was being waged at low level as the *Geschwader* carried out fighter-bomber and ground-attack missions against the Soviet Army, and its lines of supply.

Targets were plentiful – concentrations of troops and armour, rail communications and road convoys. And, of course, now that winter had once again brought shipping to a standstill, traffic on the 'ice road' across Lake Ladoga. One of the most successful exponents of the low-level attack was Oberleutnant Edwin Dutel. Nicknamed the '*Jabo* King', Dutel, the *Gruppen*-Adjutant of I./JG 54, led his own special *Jabo-Schwarm* .

Among the many weapons used against the 'ice road' were oil bombs (filled with a mixture of petroleum and high explosive) and large-calibre demolition bombs. But the holes melted by the former quickly froze over again, and the surface damage caused by the latter could be easily circumnavigated.

More effective were the small 2 kg (4.4-lb) SD-2 'Butterfly' bombs, which had been employed in large numbers against ground targets at the start of *Barbarossa*. Scattered repeatedly along the 'ice road', the white-painted SD-2s were all but invisible in the snow and, acting like minefields, caused severe disruption.

One pilot still recalls a particularly horrific incident on frozen Lake Ladoga. Under cover of darkness the Russians had cleared a narrow, but shorter, path across the ice linking the nearest section of Soviet-held shore to the Leningrad enclave.

Krasnogvardeisk, as seen from the air. A solitary Bf 109 has been left out in the cold (centre foreground) as the new Fw 190s are given pride of place on the apron in front of the hangar

Presumably it was thought that this exposed stretch could be crossed by a forced night march. But early morning reconnaissance revealed the path still packed with a seemingly endless column of troops, six abreast, heading doggedly for the western side of the lake. Fighters were called up and ordered to ground-strafe. Soon, the narrow chasm across the ice, hemmed in by snow banked high on either side, resembled a 'river of blood'.

But the latest Soviet offensive to relieve Leningrad was to be at least

With its days in the east already numbered, a III. *Gruppe Gustav* heads out on to the runway . . .

. . . its swansong drowned by the throaty roar of a BMW radial at full power. Note the difference in 'stance' of the two machines, the wide-legged undercarriage of the Fw 190 making it ideal for the more primitive conditions of the eastern front

Excellent it may have been, but invincible the Focke-Wulf was not. This is Unteroffizier Helmut Brandt's 'Black 2', forced down on the frozen surface of Lake Ladoga on 16 January 1943 and subsequently recovered by the Soviets

partially successful. The ancient fortress of Schlüsselburg on the south side of Lake Ladoga, which had been in German hands since the autumn of 1941, was recaptured and a tenuous link with the city established. Further attempts to widen this lakeside corridor failed, and the situation would remain largely unaltered until January 1944.

Even before the launch of the Soviet offensive I./JG 54 had begun re-equipping with the radial-engined Focke-Wulf 190, a sturdy bruiser of a fighter much better suited to withstanding the rigours of a Russian winter than the Bf 109. The *Gruppe* reportedly rotated back to Heiligenbeil, in East Prussia, one *Staffel* at a time to undergo conversion.

The first examples of the new fighter had flown in to Krasnogvardeisk early in January 1943, and it was not long before the first of them was lost. Unteroffizier Helmut Brandt of 2./JG 54 forced-landed on the frozen surface of Lake Ladoga close to Schlüsselburg on 16 January after tangling with four fighters of the Soviet 158th Regiment. On 1 February another pair of Focke-Wulfs were lost over the same area, with 3. *Staffel's* Oberleutnant Günther Götze and Unteroffizier Karl Kulka both being reported missing.

It was not long after this that Hauptmann Reinhard Seiler's III. *Gruppe*, which had been operating in the Smolensk region (south of the *Heeresgruppe* boundary) since December, was withdrawn from the eastern front altogether. For the remainder of the war it would operate solely against the Western allies.

On 19 February JG 54 reached another milestone when Feldwebel Otto Kittel scored the *Geschwader's* 4000th kill of the war. But, as ever, success came at a price. And 48 hours later II. *Gruppe* lost their *Kommandeur* when Major Hans Hahn's *Gustav* suffered engine (text continues on page 78)

COLOUR PLATES

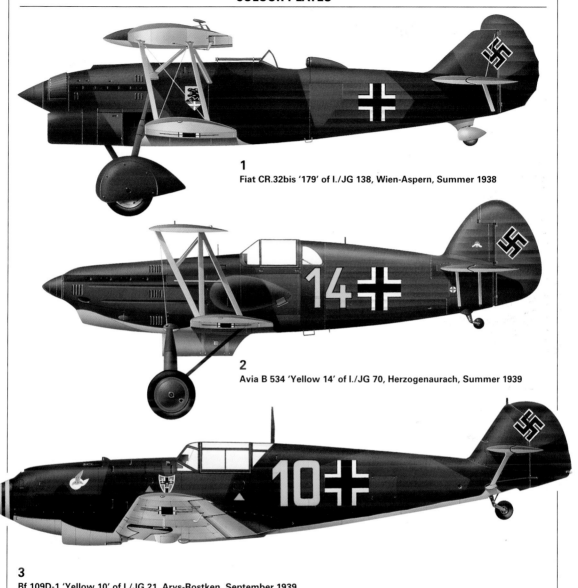

1
Fiat CR.32bis '179' of I./JG 138, Wien-Aspern, Summer 1938

2
Avia B 534 'Yellow 14' of I./JG 70, Herzogenaurach, Summer 1939

3
Bf 109D-1 'Yellow 10' of I./JG 21, Arys-Rostken, September 1939

4
Bf 109E-1 'White 2' of I./JG 76, Stubendorf, September 1939

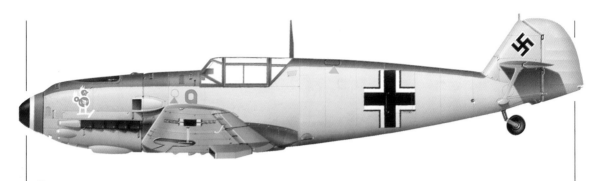

5
Bf 109E-1 'Red 9' of I./JG 21, Le Mans, Summer 1940

6
Bf 109E-1 'White 11' of III./JG 54, Guines-South, August 1940

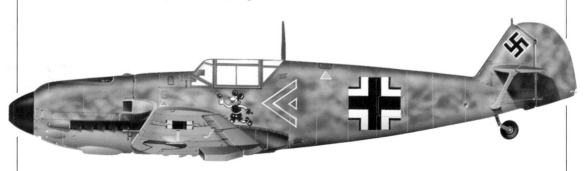

7
Bf 109E-3 'White Double Chevron' of Hauptmann Hubertus von Bonin, *Gruppenkommandeur* I./JG 54, Campagne-les-Guines, September 1940

8
Bf 109E-4 'White 1' of Oberleutnant Hans Philipp, *Staffelkapitän* 4./JG 54, Campagne-les-Guines, October 1940

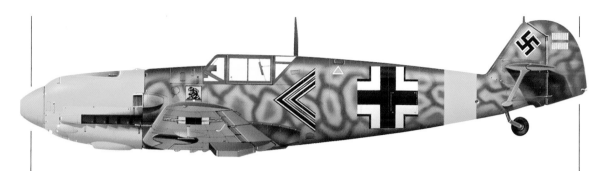

9
Bf 109E-4 'Black Double Chevron' of Hauptmann Dietrich Hrabak, *Gruppenkommandeur* I./JG 54, Graz-Thalerhof, April 1941

10
Bf 109F-2 'Yellow 1' of Oberleutnant Hans Schmoller-Haldy, *Staffelkapitän* 4./JG 54, Sarudinye, August 1941

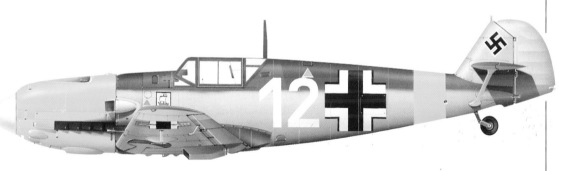

11
Bf 109E-7 'White 12' of 1.(Eins)/JG 54, Windau, September 1941

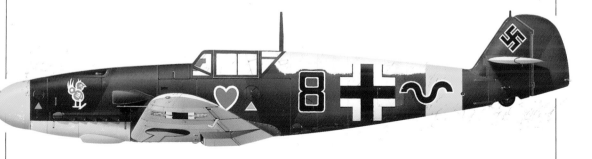

12
Bf 109F-2 'Black 8' of III./JG 54, Siverskaya, November 1941

13
Bf 109F-2 'Black Chevron and Bars' of Hauptmann Hans Philipp, *Gruppenkommandeur* I./JG 54,
Krasnogvardeisk, March 1942

14
Bf 109F-2 'Black 8' of Feldwebel Otto Kittel, I./JG 54, Krasnogvardeisk, May 1942

15
Bf 109F-4 'White Double Chevron' of Hauptmann Reinhard Seiler, *Gruppenkommandeur* III./JG 54,
Siverskaya, Summer 1942

16
Bf 109F-2 'White 8' of Leutnant Walter Nowotny, 1./JG 54, Ryelbitzi, Summer 1942

17
Bf 109G-2 'White Chevron and Bars' of Major Hannes Trautloft, *Geschwaderkommodore* JG 54, Siverskaya, Summer 1942

18
Bf 109G-2/R6 'Yellow 7' of II./JG 54, Zhitomir, February 1943

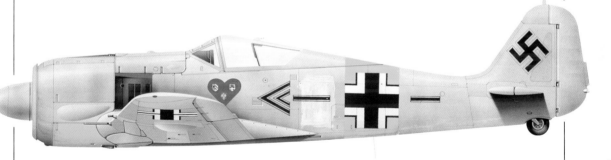

19
Fw 190A-4 'Black Chevron and Bars' of Oberstleutnant Hannes Trautloft, *Geschwaderkommodore* JG 54, Krasnogvardeisk, February 1943

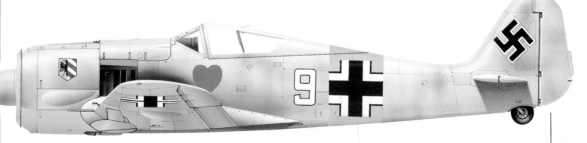

20
Fw 190A-4 'White 9' of Feldwebel Karl Schnörrer, I./JG 54, Krasnogvardeisk, February 1943

21
Fw 190A-4 'White 10' of Leutnant Walter Nowotny, *Staffelkapitän* 1./JG 54, Krasnogvardeisk, Spring 1943

22
Fw 190A-4 'White 2' of Oberfeldwebel Anton Döbele, I./JG 54, Krasnogvardeisk, Spring 1943

23
Fw 190A-5 'Black 5' of Oberleutnant Max Stotz, II./JG 54, Siverskaya, late Spring 1943

24
Bf 109G-4/R6 'Black 6' of III./JG 54, Oldenburg, May 1943

25
Fw 190A-5 'Black 7' of Leutnant Emil Lang, II./JG 54, Siverskaya, May 1943

26
Fw 190A-5 'Black 12' of Fähnrich Norbert Hannig, 5./JG 54, Siverskaya, circa May 1943

27
Fw 190A-6 'White 12' of Leutnant Helmut Wettstein, *Staffelkapitän* 1./JG 54, Shatalovka-East, September 1943

28
Fw 190A-6 'Black Double Chevron' of Hauptmann Walter Nowotny, *Gruppenkommandeur* I./JG 54, Vitebsk, November 1943

29
Bf 109G-6 'Yellow 1' of Oberleutnant Wilhelm Schilling, *Staffelkapitän* 9./JG 54, Ludwigslust, February 1944

30
Fw 190A-8 'Black 5' of III./JG 54, Villacoublay, June 1944

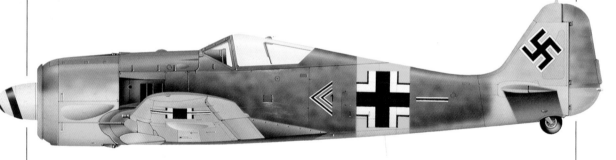

31
Fw 190A-6 'Black Double Chevron' of Hauptmann Erich Rudorffer, *Gruppenkommandeur* II./JG 54, Immola, June 1944

32
Fw 190A-8 'White 3' of Oberleutnant Karl Brill, *Staffelkapitän* 10./JG 54, Lublin, July 1944

33
Fw 190A-6 'White Chevron and Bars' of Oberstleutnant Anton Mader, *Geschwaderkommodore* JG 54,
Dorpat, Estonia, July 1944

34
Fw 190A-6 'Yellow 5' of Oberleutnant Otto Kittel, I./JG 54, Riga-Skulte, September 1944

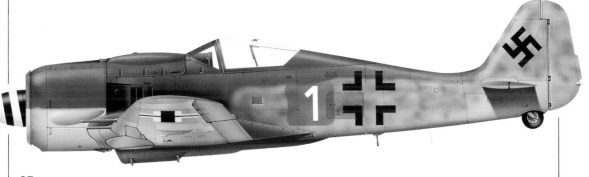

35
Fw 190A-8 'White 1' of Leutnant Heinz Wernicke, *Staffelkäpitan* 1./JG 54, Riga-Spilve, September 1944

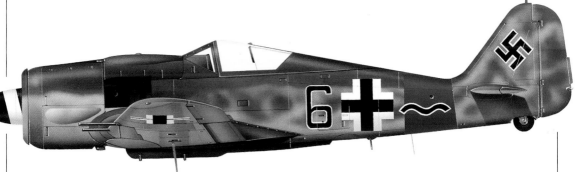

36
Fw 190A-8 'Black 6' of IV./JG 54, Mörtitz, November 1944

37
Fw 190A-8 'Black Double Chevron' of Hauptmann Franz Eisenach, *Gruppenkommandeur* I./JG 54, Schrunden, November 1944

38
Fw 190A-8 'White 12' of Oberleutnant Josef Heinzeller, *Staffelkapitän* 1./JG 54, Schrunden, December 1944

39
Fw 190D-9 'Black 4' of III./JG 54, Varrelbusch, December 1944

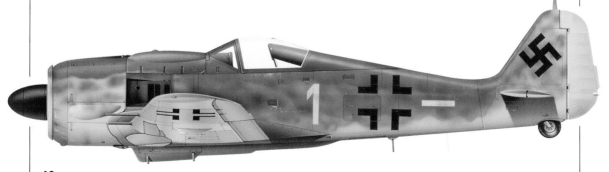

40
Fw 190A-9 'Yellow 1' of Hauptmann Helmut Wettstein, *Staffelkapitän* 6./JG 54, Libau-Nord, February 1945

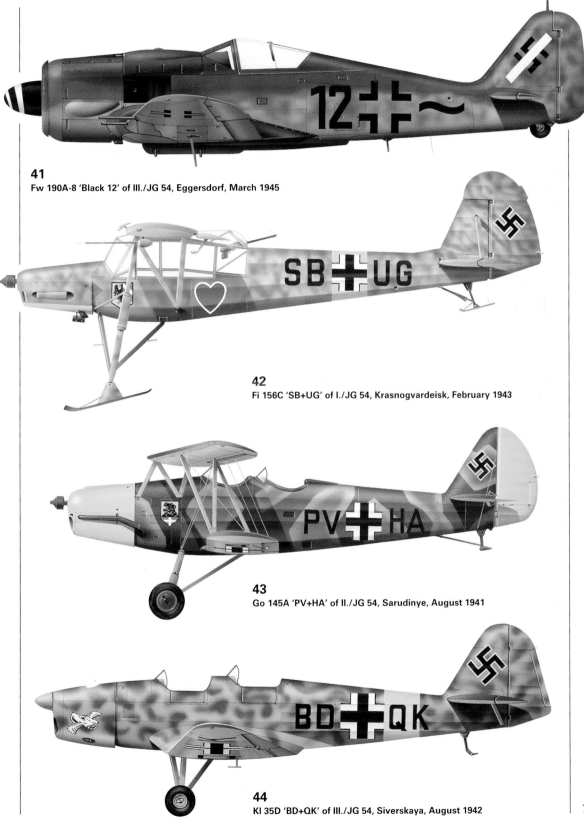

41
Fw 190A-8 'Black 12' of III./JG 54, Eggersdorf, March 1945

42
Fi 156C 'SB+UG' of I./JG 54, Krasnogvardeisk, February 1943

43
Go 145A 'PV+HA' of II./JG 54, Sarudinye, August 1941

44
Kl 35D 'BD+QK' of III./JG 54, Siverskaya, August 1942

1
JG 54 *'Grünherz'*
worn below the cockpit on the
Bf 109E, F and G, and the Fw 190A

2
I./JG 54
worn below the windscreen on the
Bf 109E, F and G, and on the cowling
of the Fw 190A

3
1./JG 54
worn below the cockpit on the
Bf 109E/F

4
2./JG 54
worn below the windscreen on the
Bf 109E and on the cowling of the
Fw 190A

5
3./JG 54
worn below the cockpit on the
Bf 109E/F

6
II./JG 54
worn below the windscreen on the
Fiat CR.32, Bf 109C, D, E, F and G,
and on the cowling of the Fw 190A

7
III./JG 54
worn on the cowling or below the
windscreen of the Bf 109D, E, F and G,
and below the cockpit of the Fw 190A

8
7./JG 54 (1940-42)
worn on the cowling of the Bf 109E,
F and G

9
7./JG 54 (1942-43)
worn on the cowling of the Bf 109G

10
8./JG 54 (ex-2./JG 21)
worn on the cowling of the Bf 109D,
E, F and G

11
9./JG 54
worn on the cowling of the Bf 109E,
F and G

12
IV./JG 54 (1943-44)
possibly worn below the windscreen
of the Bf 109G

13
IV./JG 54 (1944)
worn on the cowling of the Fw 190A

14
10./JG 54 (later 13.)
worn below the cockpit of the
Fw 190A

15
3./JG 21
worn on the cowling of the
Bf 109D/E

16
I./JG 54
personal emblem of Hauptmann
Hubertus von Bonin

17
1./JG 54
personal emblem of Oberleutnant
Reinhard Seiler

18
III./JG 54
personal emblem of Leutnant
Erwin Leykauf

19 February 1943, and yet more celebrations, this time to mark the *Geschwader's* 4000th victory of the war – note the running total in the 'Green Heart' top left! At the table from left to right, Feldwebel Otto Kittel, Major Hannes Trautloft and Hauptmann Hans Philipp

failure, and he was forced to land in thick woods behind enemy lines near the Demyansk salient (the evacuation of which had commenced this very day).

'Assi' Hahn's natural ebullience was a watchword throughout the *Jagdwaffe*. He would need all the fortitude and inner strength he possessed to survive the next seven years of Soviet captivity. Shortly after being taken prisoner he was introduced to Soviet Marshal Timoshenko, but there the civilities ended. He attempted to escape from the Borovichi PoW camp in April, for which he was sentenced to death by a Gorki court in August. Hahn subsequently spent months in a death cell in Moscow's Lubyanka prison before being reprieved, but still refused the blandishments of the 'National Committee of Free Germany', an organisation of ex-*Wehrmacht* prisoners dedicated to working on the side of the Soviets.

In June 1944 Hans Hahn was sent to the infamous Block VI of the Yelabuga prison camp. During the closing weeks of the war he was first tortured, and then hospitalised, by the NKVD. He was eventually repatriated to Germany just before Christmas 1949.

The man chosen to replace 'Assi' Hahn at the head of II./JG 54 was the erstwhile *Kapitän* of his 4. *Staffel*, Hauptmann Heinrich Jung, who had joined the 'Green Hearts' in November 1940. Less than a fortnight later another of Hahn's *Staffelkapitäne*, who had likewise been with the *Geschwader* since the autumn of 1940, was lost. Oberleutnant Hans Beisswenger of 6./JG 54 took off at the head of his *Schwarm* on 6 March for a *Freie Jagd* sweep along the Staraya Russa-Kholm highway south of Lake Ilmen. Leading the second *Rotte* was Unteroffizier Georg Munderloh;

'Arriving over our designated operational area, I sighted 15 Il-2s escorted by some 15-20 LaGG-3s. I reported the enemy aircraft to Beiss-wenger. We were converging head

Major Hans Hahn shoehorns his ample frame into the narrow cockpit of his *Gustav*. It was in this machine – or one bearing identical markings – that 'Assi' Hahn forced-landed behind Soviet lines on 21 February 1943 to begin nearly seven long years of captivity

on at very high speed. My *Rotte* was slightly in the lead, with Beisswenger and his wingman above us and off to one side. I requested and received permission to commence the attack. I managed to shoot down a LaGG-3 on my first pass, which Beisswenger confirmed over the R/T. Then he must have become involved in the fight himself, for I heard or saw nothing further of him.'

Munderloh downed another LaGG (his 20th kill) during a second pass, but was then involved in a mid-air collision with a third enemy machine. With his engine dead, he had no choice but to land in enemy-occupied territory. Taken prisoner, he was later told by Soviet pilots involved in the action that they had shot down another German fighter.

That could only have been Beisswenger. After claiming two of the LaGG-3s – which took his final total to 152 – he had been set upon by ten others. His 'Yellow 4' was last seen at low level, its engine turning slowly, as he tried to make it back to the German lines.

Meanwhile, I. *Gruppe* had been busy proving the superiority of its new Focke-Wulfs. On 23 February 34 Soviet aircraft were claimed for no loss. Seven had gone to *Kommandeur* Hans Philipp, raising his score to 180. On 7 March, by which time it, too, had transferred from the stalemate of the Leningrad front down to Staraya Russa, I./JG 54 was even more successful, being credited with 59 enemy aircraft destroyed, again without loss.

Among the claimants were Hans Götz (for his 63rd) and Walter Nowotny (66th). The *Geschwaderstab's* Fw 190s were also aloft that day, allowing *Kommodore* Hannes Trautloft to down his 53rd. But all were put in the shade, once again, by 'Fips' Philipp, whose nine victories increased his personal tally to 189.

On 14 March two more names were added to JG 54's growing list of Knight's Cross recipients. Oberfeldwebel Herbert Broennle,

. . . but some things are best done the old way. And in Russia the panje pony, whether pulling a cart in summer or a sledge in winter, was an integral and indispensable part of everyday life

Within weeks of their arrival, I. *Gruppe's* previously pristine Fw 190s were looking every bit as grubby and worn as the *Gustavs* they had replaced. This photograph shows Krasnogvardeisk's crowded dispersal early in 1943

Grubby perhaps, but lethal too! On 7 March I./JG 54's Fw 190s were credited with no fewer than 59 Soviet aircraft destroyed. Among that day's claimants was Leutnant Walter Nowotny, *Kapitän* of 1. *Staffel*, whose 'White 1' is seen here returning from an earlier mission. Note the obvious signs of previous ownership – the deletion of a higher numeral ahead of the fuselage cross and of a II. *Gruppe* horizontal bar behind

who had joined 4. *Staffel* during the Battle of Britain, and had since been seriously wounded over Leningrad, was honoured for his 57 kills to date. Broennle would add just one more, an American B-24, before being killed over Sicily on 4 July as a member of 2./JG 53.

The other award, for 46 victories, went to Oberleutnant Günther Fink, Trautloft's second most successful 'nightfighter' of 1942, who was now *Kapitän* of 8. *Staffel* on the western front. He, too, was soon to lose his life in action against US 'heavies' (B-17s of the Eighth Air Force) over the North Sea on 15 May.

But Hans Philipp's progress was seemingly unstoppable. On 17 March – his 26th birthday – four more victories took his total to 203. This made him the highest-scoring fighter pilot in the entire Luftwaffe! JG 52's Hermann Graf, the first to reach the 200-mark on 2 October 1942, had immediately been taken off operations and had not scored since.

On 1 April 'Fips' Philipp was appointed *Kommodore* of JG 1, the premier Defence of the Reich *Geschwader*. There, a very different kind of war awaited him. As he was later to write in a letter to his great friend, and erstwhile *Kommodore* back at JG 54, Hannes Trautloft;

'Facing up to 200 Russians eager to have a nibble at you, or even Spitfires, can be quite enjoyable . . . but curve in against 70 Boeing Fortresses and all your past sins flash before your eyes.'

They were prophetic words. After claiming a B-17 – his 206th, and final victory – Oberstleutnant Hans Philipp would be killed in action against US escort fighters on 8 October.

Upon Philipp's departure from I./JG 54, Hauptmann Reinhard Seiler had relinquished command of III./JG 54 in the west and returned to the Russian front to replace him at the head of I. *Gruppe*. 'Seppl' Seiler's

arrival coincided with a period of unseasonably bad spring weather over the northern sector.

The main activity on the ground was currently along the central front, where the Soviets had just recaptured the important bastion of Vyazma, and thus removed the last threat to Moscow. But I. and II./JG 54 continued to fly over the Leningrad area whenever conditions allowed.

April was to witness the usual mix of fortunes. Among the month's losses was '*Jabo* King' Edwin Dutel, shot down during a low-level mission south-east of Schlüsselburg on the

9th. Exactly one week later Leutnant Hans Ademeit was awarded the Knight's Cross for achieving 53 victories. Ademeit had first joined the *Geschwader* back in 1940. Like several other long-serving members of the 'Green Hearts', most notably perhaps Otto Kittel, Ademeit had found success hard to come by while flying the Bf 109. It was only after conversion to the Fw 190 that his true skills became apparent, and his score rose.

April also saw another brief deployment to Finland. The object of the exercise on this occasion, however, was not to attack supply shipping on Lake Ladoga, but to patrol the anti-submarine net across the mouth of the Gulf of Finland.

This barrier stretched from Reval (Tallinn), in Estonia, to Porkkala on the Finnish coast west of Helsinki. It had been laid during the previous winter to keep all Soviet submarines bottled up in the Gulf, and prevent their emerging into the main Baltic basin, where they would not only be a danger to German and Finnish convoys, but would also pose a threat to the *Kriegsmarine's* own U-boat training areas.

The *Schwarm* of 5. *Staffel Gustavs* selected to carry out this task quickly settled in to a routine of its own. After a hard day spent patrolling the net, and safeguarding it from Soviet interference, pilots usually contrived to

I. *Gruppe* parade to bid farewell to their *Kommandeur* as Hauptmann Hans Philipp (right) departs to assume command of JG 1 in Defence of the Reich. Hannes Trautloft, who would himself soon be leaving the 'Green Hearts', addresses the assembled company

An Fw 190 fighter-bomber of I./JG 54's special *Jaboschwarm*. It was in a machine similar to this ('White 1 – or 'I'?) that the *Schwarmführer, Gruppen*-Adjutant Oberleutnant Edwin Dutel – the '*Jabo* King' – was reported missing near Schlüsselburg on 9 April

stay overnight at Helsinki's modern Malmi airport, officially opened less than five years earlier, and just a short taxi-ride away from the delights of the Finnish capital.

Helsinki's nightlife was far removed from the minds of most I. and II. *Gruppe* pilots, however. Their daily lot was the constant battle against the growing might of the Red Air Force. Russian air attacks continued unabated. But as Soviet ground activity in the northern area slackened off in May, *Luftflotte* 1 began to turn its attention to the enemy's rear-area lines of supply.

These *Gustavs* of 5. *Staffel* are seen parked in Finland in April 1943. No signs of the pilots, though. Could this be the perimeter track at Malmi – and could they be already on their way to the fleshpots of the Finnish capital?

JG 54's fighters thus found themselves also escorting Gen Korten's remaining bomber and dive-bomber forces, now reduced to a meagre 80-odd He 111s of KG 53 and half that number of Ju 87s (of I./StG 5), as they attacked Soviet railway lines and depots beyond the Volkhov. Supply shipping on Lake Ladoga, and the harbours along its southern and eastern shores, were also prime targets.

And it was over one of the latter targets, Novaya Ladoga, that the *Staffelkapitän* of 1./JG 54, Oberleutnant Walter Nowotny, claimed his century on 15 June. Nine days later two *Freie Jagd* sweeps along the Volkhov netted him another ten victories, raising his overall total to 124.

Nowotny, together with Max Stotz, was immediately ordered to take six weeks enforced home leave. His 'sore throat' (Luftwaffe slang to describe the keenness shown by some for high decorations to hang around their necks) apparently no better after his belated Knight's Cross, Nowotny noted somewhat miffily in his combat record book before departure, 'Waiting for the Oak Leaves, waiting in vain'.

By mid-June Hauptmann Jung's II. *Gruppe* had also completed conversion on to the Fw 190. Meanwhile, efforts to sever the Soviet's lines of supply to the Leningrad front were still the priority. Among the most important targets were the railway bridges across the Volkhov, which now lay some 30 miles (50 km) behind the frontlines. Attempts to destroy these vital bottlenecks by heavy railway guns hidden in the woods around Mga had proved fruitless. *Luftflotte* 1 was therefore given the task of knocking out the bridges.

A series of raids were flown, the first by the Stukas of I./StG 5 covered by just two *Schwärme* of Focke-Wulfs. But they steadily increased in strength and intensity as each post-mission reconnaissance sortie revealed the bridges still to be intact.

The Russians were equally aware of the importance of this artery. It is estimated that some 1000 anti-aircraft guns of every calibre ringed the target area by the time of the eighth and final attack. This was flown by every aircraft available to *Luftflotte* 1 and was escorted by both *Gruppen* of JG 54. 'Everybody was roped in', one participant dryly noted, 'just like the Reich's annual Party Day celebrations, only not quite so much fun!'

5. *Staffel's* Fähnrich Norbert Hannig, a recent arrival from 2./EJGr-West at Biarritz, and no relation to the Horst Hannig mentioned earlier, was one of those involved;

'I was flying wingman to Xaver (Feldwebel Xaver Müller), an experienced and successful *Schwarmführer*, acting as close support to the leading He 111s. From our position, weaving gently just above and ahead of the bombers, we could clearly see the crews bathed in bright sunlight behind the glass of their canopies as we approached the target from the south at an altitude of 5000 metres (16,500 ft). Ahead of us, some 2000 metres (6500 ft) lower, were the Ju 87s.

'But just before the dive-bombers could commence their attack a veritable inferno of flak opened up. Tracers spun fiery webs and large calibre shells exploded in black mushrooms of smoke which drifted down to form an unbroken carpet of dirty cloud into which the Stukas dived and disappeared.

'As our bombers came within range, the barrage rose to meet us – enveloping black smoke, the flash of explosions, the stink of cordite strong even through our oxygen masks. The sun turned blood-red, as if seen through smoked glass. The Heinkels, even Xaver alongside me – crystal clear a moment earlier – were just dim silhouettes in the murky darkness.'

But suddenly they were through – back into brilliant sunshine, the bombers still in formation. Despite the Soviet fire, losses were minimal. And, as reconnaissance was to confirm, one span of the bridge had been hit and had collapsed into the river. The supply trains continued to roll towards Leningrad, however. The mystery was solved a few days later;

'In between our raids, the Soviets had been busy laying a spur line which connected to an underwater bridge some seven kilometres (four miles) downstream! But as the bombers were needed elsewhere, further attacks had to be called off.'

The 'elsewhere' was the central sector, where the Luftwaffe was gathering to support Operation *Zitadelle*, the imminent offensive against the Kursk salient. By early July most of *Luftflotte 1*'s units had been transferred to the control of *Luftflotte 6*. This included I./JG 54, which moved down to Orel on the northern shoulder of the salient.

Many regard the annihilation of the German 6. *Armee* at Stalingrad in the winter of 1942-43 as the turning point of the war on the eastern front. But it was the confrontation at Kursk the following summer – resulting in the greatest tank battle in the history of warfare, before it was prematurely broken off on the express orders of the Führer – that effectively saw the *Wehrmacht* transformed from an invading force into one increasingly beset by defeat and withdrawals, ultimately ending among the ruins of Berlin.

Zitadelle was launched on 5 July. Flying a combination of *Freie Jagd* and fighter-escort sorties, I. *Gruppe's* 20+ serviceable Fw 190s claimed a significant number of victories along the northern flank of the salient. But the 11-day battle, which was terminated on 15 July, cost I./JG 54 nine pilots killed or missing, plus another two wounded.

Gruppenkommandeur Major Reinhard Seiler claimed his century on the second day of operations, but was himself forced to bail out seriously wounded near Ponyri, midway between Orel and Kursk. Although he made a good recovery, 'Seppl' Seiler was classified as unfit for further combat flying. In March 1944 he would be awarded the Oak Leaves for his 100 confirmed kills, and five months later was appointed *Kommodore* of a training *Geschwader*, JG 104, which he would lead until its disbandment in April 1945.

Major Reinhard Seiler, whose injuries on the second day of *Zitadelle* brought his long service with JG 54 to an end. As well as being twice seriously wounded – during the Battle of Britain and at Kursk – 'Seppl' Seiler must have sustained at least one more injury at some time, for this earlier portrait of him as a hauptmann shows him wearing the 'wound badge' in silver (below the Iron Cross on his left breast), which was normally awarded to members of the *Wehrmacht* who had been wounded three or four times

D.(Luft) 5001

Horrido

DES JÄGERS SCHIESSFIBEL

TRAUTLOFT 44

Oberstleutnant Hannes Trautloft's appointment as *Inspizient Ost* did not mean a complete severing of his ties with JG 54. Indeed, he kept in close touch with the *Geschwader* he had led for close on three years. And he took with him into his new office of *Inspizient* the qualities that had made him such an outstanding *Kommodore* – care and concern for those serving under him. He even designed, and drew the cover for, the 1944 publication *Horrido des Jägers Schiessfibel* (*Tally-Ho! A Shooting Primer for Fighter Pilots*). This official RLM document – D.(Luft) 5001 – was clearly marked 'Not to be taken on operations!' And no wonder . . .

. . . if this illustration explaining the principles of 'leading' a target is anything to go by! The drawings are self-explanatory. The two lines of doggerel below translate roughly as 'The fighter pilot always prefers the direct approach'. D.(Luft) 5001 is very different from the comparable AirMin pamphlet on the same subject. What a simple Soviet *apparatchik* would have made of it beggars belief!

On 8 July Oberleutnant Franz Eisenach, who had originally been a *Zerstörer* pilot before transferring to the *Jagdwaffe*, and then becoming *Staffelkapitän* of 3./JG 54 in May 1943, was also wounded. His injuries proving less severe than Seiler's, he was soon back at the head of his *Staffel*. But he would be wounded again in December, which would keep him off operations for the following six months. Returning to I. *Gruppe* in the summer of 1944, he would serve as its *Kommandeur* for the last nine months of the war.

Two days after the abandonment of *Zitadelle*, on 17 July, I. *Gruppe's* Feldwebel Helmut Missner was credited with JG 54's 5000th kill of the war. Although nearly as many victories again were still to be claimed in the coming final twenty-two months of hostilities, Missner's achievement marked a watershed. Henceforth the *Geschwader*, like the *Wehrmacht* in general, would find itself increasingly on the defensive.

But it was another event less than a fortnight earlier which had, perhaps, been more of a true turning point for the 'Green Hearts'. Oberstleutnant Trautloft who, with his *Geschwaderstab* and II. *Gruppe*, had remained on the northern sector during the Kursk offensive, had relinquished command of JG 54 on 6 July to become *Inspizient Ost* (Inspector East) on the staff of *General der Jagdflieger* Adolf Galland.

As the one man more than any other who had imprinted his personality and name upon the unit (JG 54 was often referred to as the '*Jagdgeschwader* Trautloft'), Hannes Trautloft would continue to maintain close links with the 'Green Hearts' in the difficult days ahead. But his departure was more than the closing of a chapter. It was the passing of an era.

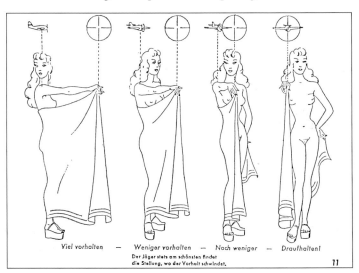

Viel vorhalten — Weniger vorhalten — Noch weniger — Draufhalten!

Der Jäger steht am schönsten findet die Stellung, wo der Vorhalt schwindet.

11

'GREEN HEARTS' IN THE WEST

Before charting the long months of retreat and defeat in the east, mention must be made of III./JG 54's operations against the Western Allies. After the *Gruppe's* withdrawal from the Russian front early in 1943, it was initially deployed for some months on a semi-autonomous basis in the Reich, before coming increasingly under the control of JG 26.

As such, its later history is more rightly part of the JG 26 story. In fact, III./JG 54 would be redesignated and officially incorporated into the latter *Geschwader* as IV./JG 26 in February 1945. But as the *Gruppe's* fighters continued to sport the 'Green Heart' badge throughout much of this period, and its members – in the early days, at least – retained an obvious affinity with their parent *Geschwader* in Russia, its activities against the RAF and USAAF form an integral part of the overall history.

III./JG 54's withdrawal from Russia was the result of a decision by Adolf Galland, the *General der Jagdflieger*, to exchange one complete western-based *Jagdgeschwader* with another from the eastern front. The two units selected were JGs 26 and 54. Although both were highly experienced, each had gained their expertise in their own specific theatre of operations, which was very different from the other's. Consequently, both would require a certain period of 'acclimatisation' before becoming fully effective in their new environments.

In retrospect, it is not quite clear what Galland hoped to achieve by this arbitrary exchange at such a sensitive juncture of the war on the two fronts (in the aftermath of Stalingrad, the Soviets were beginning to gain the ascendancy in the east, while in the west the US Eighth Air Force had just embarked upon its daylight bombing offensive against the Reich). In fairness, the two *Jagdgeschwader* were not to be transferred en bloc, but rather a *Gruppe* at a time in order to keep the inevitable disruption to a minimum.

But either Galland thought better of it – or more cautious minds prevailed upon him so to do – for the scheme was abandoned after just one *Gruppe*, plus one additional *Staffel*, from each *Jagdgeschwader* had made the move. And whereas those units of JG 26 which had been transferred to Russia would return to the Channel front after some four months of campaigning against the Soviets, for the members of JG 54 involved in the exchange the move to the west was to prove permanent.

At the beginning of February 1943 III./JG 54, led by *Gruppenkommandeur* Hauptmann Reinhard Seiler, left Smolensk, on the central sector of the eastern front, by train for Lille-Vendeville, in northern France. At about the same time 4./JG 54, under *Staffelkapitän* Oberleutnant Siegfried Graf von Matuschka, departed Krasnogvardeisk – also by rail – for Wevelghem, in Belgium. Here, the latter would operate as part of III./JG 26, now minus its 7. *Staffel* which had entrained for the east some two weeks earlier.

Meanwhile, after arriving at Lille-Vendville on 12 February, the pilots of III./JG 54 were flown by Ju 52 transport to Wiesbaden to collect their new Bf 109G-4s. Upon their return they were subjected to an intense period of training designed to prepare them for Channel front operations. This was carried out under the critical eye of Major Josef 'Pips' Priller, the *Kommodore* of JG 26, whose *Geschwaderstab* was also occupying Lille-Vendeville.

It quickly became apparent that 'Seppl' Seiler's eastern front *Experten*, more used to operating at low-level in individual *Schwarm* or *Rotte* strength against the Soviet air force, were ill-suited to take their place alongside JGs 2 and 26 as part of the Luftwaffe first line of defence in the west. The Channel-based *Jagdgeschwader* had evolved their own set of skills necessary to combat not only the Anglo-American fighter and medium bomber forces, but also the growing numbers of high-flying US 'heavies'.

Despite their best efforts, the perfectionist Major Priller steadfastly refused to declare III./JG 54 operational. It was his negative reports to higher authority which allegedly drove the final nail into the coffin of Adolf Galland's exchange scheme.

During the *Gruppe's* six weeks of Channel front familiarisation, it had suffered close on a dozen Bf 109s lost or damaged from a variety of accidental causes but, as far as is known, only one combat fatality – 7. *Staffel's* Unteroffizier Erich Twelkemeyer was reported missing after a dogfight near Boulogne on 26 February. Just over four weeks later, on 27 March 1943, III./JG 54 was transferred to Oldenburg, in northern Germany. Here, beyond the then range of Allied single-engined fighters, the *Gruppe* would spend the next three months concentrating solely on Defence of the Reich duties.

While III. *Gruppe* had been engaged in its ultimately abortive period of Channel front training, two other *Staffeln* bearing the designation of JG 54 had been actively employed against the western Allies. These units' association with the 'Green Hearts' was, however, both brief and tenuous in the extreme. Each of the two Channel *Jagdgeschwader* (JGs 2 and 26) had long controlled two separate specialist *Staffeln* apiece – a 10.(*Jabo*) fighter-bomber *Staffel*, and an 11. high-altitude fighter *Staffel* equipped with pressurised Bf 109G-1s.

A bomb-laden Fw 190 of 10.(*Jabo*)/JG 54 leaves its camouflaged dispersal at St Omer-Wizernes for another hit-and-run raid in southern England early in 1943

In late January 1943 the Fw 190s of 10.(*Jabo*)/JG 26 based at St Omer-Wisernes had been redesignated 10.(*Jabo*)/JG 54. As a dedicated cross-Channel fighter-bomber unit, this *Staffel* was presumably considered unsuitable for transfer to Russia, and its re-numbering was simply an early move in Galland's exchange plans pending the arrival of the main body of JG 54 from the eastern front. To signify their new allegiance, the *Staffel's* pilots were reportedly instructed to remove their JG 26 *'Schlageter'* cuff titles – although in reality they continued to operate, as before, under the control of their erstwhile parent *Geschwader*.

A photograph taken by one of the low-flying attackers during the devastating raid on Ashford, in Kent, on 24 March, which killed 50 and wounded 77. According to one source, the puff of white smoke just visible in the distance in the centre of this shot marks the spot where the remains of Oberleutnant Paul 'Bomben' Keller's 'Black 7' hit the ground – his machine had exploded in mid-air when its 500-kg (1100-lb) bomb was detonated, either by a direct hit from an anti-aircraft shell or from fragments thrown up during his strafing run

Likewise, a specialised high-altitude fighter *Staffel* had little useful part to play on the Russian front, where the Red Air Force operated predominantly at low-level. Consequently, when 11./JG 26 (which had been disbanded in December 1942) was resuscitated at Merville in February 1943, it was given the designation 11./JG 54.

For three months these *Staffeln* conducted their operations under the banner of JG 54. For the Focke-Wulfs of 10.(*Jabo*) *Staffel* this meant a continuation of the sporadic cross-Channel fighter-bomber raids against targets in southern England which they had been mounting of late. After losing Feldwebel Emil Bösch on 12 March, shot down by an RAF Typhoon some six miles (10 km) off Dunkirk, the *Staffel* caused significant damage during a mid-morning attack on Ashford, in Kent, on 24 March. Casualties on the ground were heavy, but the town's anti-aircraft defences claimed one success, hitting the machine of *Staffelkampitän* Oberleutnant Paul Keller, which exploded in mid-air.

Five days later Unteroffizier Joachim Koch fell victim to a Spitfire over Brighton. And three more pilots of 10.(*Jabo*)/JG 54 would be reported missing over the Channel before the unit, commanded now by Oberleutnant Erwin Busch, underwent a second redesignation in mid-April 1943, this time to become part of *Schnellkapfgeschwader* 10.

Less is known of 11./JG 54's high-altitude activities out of Merville during this period. After writing-off a couple of Bf 109G-1s in take-off and landing accidents, the *Staffel* began to receive new pressurised G-3s. By early May, however, its high-level role appears to have been abandoned for the unit had transferred to Wevelghem, in Belgium, where it re-equipped with Fw 190s. On 21 May 11./JG 54 scored its only recorded success when Oberfeldwebel Reinheld Hoffmann downed a P-47 low over the Belgian coast near Blankenberge. Before the month was out the *Staffel* was reportedly disbanded, most of its members being reincorporated into JG 26.

Meanwhile, the pilots of Hauptmann Reinhard Seiler's III./JG 54, no doubt still smarting from being adjudged not proficient enough for Channel front operations, were cutting their teeth on the Eighth Air

Force's four-engined bombers over northern Germany. In little more than two months they claimed a creditable 28 of the American 'heavies'.

The unit's first successes occurred on 17 April during a US raid on Bremen, when the *Gruppe* was credited with three of the sixteen B-17s lost that day. III./JG 54 had a single casualty to report. Hauptmann Hans-Ekkehard Bob, the *Kapitän* of 9. *Staffel*, bailed out wounded after colliding with a Fortress. Three other Bf 109s returned to Oldenburg with minor combat damage.

The first of the three B-17s had fallen to *Gruppenkommandeur* Hauptmann Reinhard Seiler over the target area shortly after 1300 hrs. It would be the only four-engined bomber to feature in 'Seppl' Seiler's list of exactly 100 wartime kills, for he was already under orders to return to the eastern front and assume command of I./JG 54.

The *Gruppe's* previous leader, Hauptmann Hans Philipp, had arrived in the west some days earlier to take over as *Geschwaderkommodore* of JG 1.

The officer to replace Reinhard Seiler at the head of III. *Gruppe* was Hauptmann Siegfried Schnell, a long-serving member of JG 2 'Richthofen', and one of the most successful pilots on the Channel front. After contributing three B-17s to the *Gruppe's* lengthening scoreboard, 'Wumm' Schnell led III./JG 54 across the border into neighbouring Holland on 23 June.

Based first at Arnhem-Deelen, and then at Amsterdam-Schiphol from 24 July, the *Gruppe* was now back within range of the RAF. As well as continuing to bring down the occasional US 'heavy' – the leading *Viermot-Experte* during this period was 8. *Staffel's* Oberleutnant Rudolf Patzak, who claimed seven B-17s between May and July – III./JG 54 also began to get the measure of Fighter Command.

Its main protagonists were Spitfires and Typhoons, and Hauptmann Schnell brought down a brace of each on 25 July, with a third Spitfire falling to 9. *Staffel's* Oberfeldwebel Eugen Zweigart.

Schnell and Zweigart were in action again 48 hours later, the former adding another Typhoon to his score and the latter being credited with a twin-engined Ventura. 27 July was, in fact, to prove the most successful day of III./JG 54's two-month sojourn in the Netherlands. In the space of little more than fifteen minutes they downed seven RAF machines over the Haarlem area at the cost of three pilots wounded, one of them Hauptmann Waldemar 'Hein' Wübke – he of the nightshirt incident – now *Kapitän* of 7. *Staffel*.

On 2 August 9. *Staffel* put their low-level expertise to good use when they shot down five Beaufighters of Coastal Command that were attacking a heavily escorted convoy off the Dutch coast. But less than a fortnight later, on 15 August, III./JG 54 received orders to return to the Reich and resume its high-altitude war against the Eighth Air Force over northern Germany.

Its new base was Schwerin, some 55 miles (90 km) to the east of Hamburg. Here it would remain for much of the year, slowly completing conversion on to new Bf 109G-6s, and suffering more material damage and casualties from accidental causes than from enemy action. But on 9 October the unit was able to claim four B-17s from a force despatched against targets along Germany's Baltic seaboard.

Five days later the *Gruppe* was itself sent further afield when called upon to add its weight to the Luftwaffe fighter force opposing another

Hauptmann Reinhard Seiler takes his leave of III./JG 54 at Oldenburg in April 1943 to return to the eastern front, where he was to assume command of I. *Gruppe*. His replacement, Hauptmann Siegfried Schnell, an Oak Leaves-wearing *Experte* from JG 2 'Richthofen', stands behind him

deep-penetration American raid against Schweinfurt. Of the 60 US heavy bombers which failed to return from the disastrous 'second Schweinfurt' mission on 14 October, three had been brought down by 8./JG 54 over central Germany. The *Staffel's* only fatality was Feldwebel Heinrich Bosin, who lost his life while attempting an emergency landing near Liége, in Belgium, after his fuel ran out.

At least five more pilots would be killed in action before the end of the year, including two on 29 November when the *Gruppe* was credited with three of the thirteen B-17s lost in a raid on Bremen. Early in December III./JG 54 moved from Schwerin to nearby Ludwigslust, some 20 miles (32 km) to the south. It would spend the next three months here.

Although the new year brought increasing success in terms of numbers of enemy aircraft destroyed, it was also to see a sharp rise in the *Gruppe's* casualty rate, with over a dozen pilots killed, and many more wounded, in the opening eight weeks of 1944 alone. The first major engagement of the year, on 11 January, resulted in the destruction of 11 B-17s without loss. The *Gruppe's* first two P-51s were also claimed on this date, although no fighters of this type (initially operated by the Ninth Air Force) were actually reported lost by the Americans.

On 1 February Hauptmann Siegfried Schnell relinquished command of III./JG 54 to take over as head of IV. *Gruppe* on the eastern front. Schnell's place was taken temporarily by acting *Kommandeur* Oberleutnant Rudolf Patzak, previously of 8. *Staffel*. On 20 February the Eighth Air Force launched its 'Big Week' sustained offensive against German industrial targets.

On that opening day III./JG 54 shot down six B-17s. Its pilots were also credited with two *Herausschüsse*. A *Herausschuss* (literally a 'shooting out') was the term used by the Luftwaffe to describe the damaging of a heavy bomber to such an extent that it was no longer capable of maintaining station within its combat box – i.e. it became a straggler, and thus an easy target for subsequent destruction. On the debit side, the *Gruppe's* casualties were two pilots killed, one missing and one wounded.

Twenty-four hours later, on 21 February, III./JG 54 had four more pilots killed in action. One of them was Oberleutnant Rudolf Patzak, who was shot down over Hildesheim. Patzak was in turn replaced by another acting *Kommandeur*, Hauptmann Rudolf Klemm, the *Staffelkapitän* of 7./JG 54.

The *Gruppe* was heavily engaged on two other days of the 'Big Week' offensive. On 22 February it claimed six B-17s plus one *Herausschuss*. Two days later its bag consisted of five B-24s (and a *Herausschuss*), a single B-17 and a pair of P-38 Lightning fighters. The cost to the unit had been one pilot wounded.

On 25 February III./JG 54 moved forward to Lüneburg, south-east of Hamburg. It was here that Hauptmann Rudolf 'Rudi' Sinner, until recently *Kommandeur* of IV. *Gruppe* on the eastern front, arrived to take command.

Hauptmann Sinner led III./G 54 in its next major engagement on 6 March. This was the day the Eighth Air Force first struck at Berlin – 730 heavy bombers, escorted and protected by an unprecedented 801 fighters, were despatched against targets in and around the capital of the Third Reich. Sinner's *Gruppe* was just one small part of the Luftwaffe's all-out

III./JG 54 lost four pilots in action against B-17s over the North Sea on 15 May 1943 – two of them Knight's Cross holders: Hauptmann Günther Fink, the *Kapitän* of 8. *Staffel*, and 7./JG 54's Leutnant Friedrich Rupp (pictured). Hit by return fire from the bombers' gunners, Rupp's 'White 2' dived vertically into the sea south-west of Heligoland. He had added just two US 'heavies' to the 50 kills which had won him his Knight's Cross in Russia

On 6 March 1944 – the day of the first US raid on Berlin – another *Kapitän* of 8./JG 54, Oberleutnant Gerhard Loos (pictured here earlier in Russia), was killed. He was attacked by P-51s south of Bremen and, although able to bail out, lost his life when he fell from his parachute

In April 1944 III./JG 54 began re-equipping with Fw 190A-8s. Like the Bf 109G-6s they replaced (see colour profile 29), the Focke-Wulfs also wore blue Defence of the Reich bands with the *Gruppe* vertical bar superimposed. Just visible beneath 'Yellow 2's' cockpit sill is the small 'Green Heart' badge bearing the 'Crusaders' Cross' shield. This is possibly the machine that Gefreiter Klaus Hunger was flying when reported missing in action against P-38s on 18 July after III. *Gruppe's* transfer to the Normandy front

response. In two separate missions III./JG 54 brought down nine B-17s (including one straggler) and a single B-24. In return it lost four pilots killed and three wounded.

Among the latter trio was 'Rudi' Sinner. Seriously wounded by return fire from a B-17 which had been knocked out of formation long before reaching the target area, Sinner managed to bail out of his blazing fighter near Bassum, to the south of Bremen.

One of the four dead was Oberleutnant Gerhard Loos, the *Staffelkapitän* of 8./JG 54. Just one month earlier, on 5 February, Loos had been the first member of III. *Gruppe* in the west to be awarded the Knight's Cross (for 85 kills, all but some half-dozen of which had been scored in Russia).

Loos' fighter was bounced by P-51s near Rheinselen after the bombers had turned for home. He, too, was able to bail out – at an altitude of about 2000 ft (600 m) – but accounts differ as to exactly what happened next. One source describes his parachute harness 'coming apart' as soon as the canopy opened. Another maintains that he deliberately released the harness some 60 ft (18 m) above the ground when he realised he was drifting into high-tension electricity cables. Gerhard Loos had achieved 92 victories at the time of his death, including at least two US 'heavies'.

Over the next six weeks the *Gruppe*, commanded by Major Werner Schroer – previously *Kommandeur* of II./JG 27, another Defence of the Reich unit – began to suffer increasing losses as Allied pressure mounted. On 23 March it managed to down five heavy bombers without apparent loss. Six days later, however, seven pilots were killed (two in a mid-air collision) for little or no return. On 8 April the destruction of a brace of B-24s and P-38s cost the *Gruppe* five dead and four wounded.

By this stage plans were in hand to convert III./JG 54 on to the Fw 190. This would entail transfer to southern Germany. But things got off to a bad start when a six-engined Me 323 transport carrying an advance party crashed on take-off from Lüneburg on 15 April. Twenty-five technical staff were killed, including nearly all of 7. *Staffel's* groundcrew specialists.

On 20 April III./JG 54's pilots flew south to Landau, in Bavaria, to begin re-equipment with Fw 190A-8s. After losing several Focke-Wulfs in accidents during conversion, the first major test on their new mounts took place on 19 May during a heavy raid on Brunswick by B-24s of the Eighth Air Force. The *Gruppe* claimed two Liberators, plus the destruction of five stragglers, and three of their P-38 fighter escort. But the engagement also resulted in the loss of five Focke-Wulfs, with one pilot killed and four wounded.

Five days later, on 24 May, the *Gruppe* was instrumental in bringing down no fewer than ten B-17s – including three *Herausschüsse* and the despatch of a straggler – plus a solitary P-51 during another Eighth Air Force raid on Berlin. It again suffered one fatality. 9. *Staffel's* Leutnant Reinhold Hoffmann was killed when his machine somersaulted as he attempted an emergency landing north-west of the capital. Hoffmann, who had scored 60 kills with III./JG 54 in Russia and had added six 'heavies' in the west since, would be awarded a posthumous Knight's Cross on 28 January 1945.

III./JG 54 had moved up to Illesheim, west of Nürnberg, on 23 May. But its stay here was to be brief. On 6 June Allied forces stormed ashore on the beaches of Normandy. An invasion of France had long been expected, and the Luftwaffe had contingency plans in place.

Upon receipt of the code words 'Dr Gustav West' ('Dr Gustav West' stood for 'Dringende Gefahr West', meaning 'Impending Danger West'), nearly every *Jagdgruppe* in Germany would transfer forward into France. Each unit had been assigned a specific airfield, and III./JG 54's destination was Villacoublay, a large pre-war base on the western outskirts of Paris. The *Gruppe* was to occupy the southern half of the airfield complex, which was cut in two by a busy main road, while the northern part housed the Bf 109s of III./JG 26.

With Major Schroer currently undergoing hospital treatment, the *Gruppe's* 15 serviceable Fw 190s departed Illesheim under the temporary leadership of Hauptmann Robert Weiss. Wearing the Knight's Cross (awarded back in March for 70 victories, to which he had since added another 30), 'Bazi' Weiss was a newcomer to the west, having spent the previous 12 months with I./JG 54 in Russia.

Staging via Cologne and Nancy, Weiss' small formation arrived at Villacoublay on the morning of 7 June. But not all had made it. A combination of enemy interference and the navigational inexpertise of most of the young pilots would result in many units completing the transfer to France in a sadly depleted state. Some were down to single figures. One *Gruppe* allegedly reported itself ready for action with a single fighter serviceable!

III./JG 54 flew its first Normandy operation in the early afternoon of 7 June. Hauptmann Weiss claimed two kills, his 101st and 102nd – a Spitfire near Caen and a P-51 over Guyancourt. Unteroffizier Otto Venjakob had also downed a Spitfire a few seconds after Weiss' first victim, but 8. *Staffel's* Oberfähnrich Erich Reiter was lost near Bayeux.

On D-Day+2 (8 June), the *Gruppe's* five victories included a P-51 apiece for Oberleutnant Alfred Teumer and Hauptmann Emil Lang, the *Staffelkapitäne* of 7. and 9./JG 54 respectively. Like 'Bazi' Weiss, 'Fred' Teumer and 'Bully' Lang were also both recent arrivals from the parent *Geschwader* in the east. Lang had been particularly successful against the Red Air Force, and was sporting the Oak Leaves for 144 Soviet kills.

This aerial shot of 'Black 10' was supposedly taken at Villacoublay, in which case the groundcrew working out in the open on the engines and radio seem remarkably unconcerned about the possibility of Allied fighter-bomber attack. By this stage of the war the enemy's air superiority was absolute, and most Luftwaffe fighters were kept carefully concealed under tree cover

Hauptmann Robert Weiss had led the *Gruppe's* Focke-Wulfs into France on D+1 (7 June), and was officially appointed *Kommandeur* on 21 July

By contrast, the third of the trio of *Staffelkapitäne*, 8./JG 54's Oberleutnant Eugen-Ludwig Zweigart, had been with III. *Gruppe* in the west for well over a year. During that time he had added some 15 kills to the 54 which had won him the Knight's Cross in Russia back in January 1943. Yet it was Zweigart who was numbered among this same 8 June's four fatalities, shot down by P-51s close to the landing beaches.

Zweigart's loss aside, the first 72 hours of Luftwaffe fighter operations over Normandy set the general pattern for the weeks ahead. Facing odds in the air which at times rose as high as 40-to-1 in the enemy's favour, it was the top-scoring *Experten*, together with the small but solid core of experienced NCO pilots, who would survive the blood-bath over France and gain the victories, while it was the inadequately trained youngsters – forming the bulk of the *Jagdwaffe* opposition to the Allied invasion – who would fill the casualty lists.

And as these lists lengthened, and new reinforcements with even less training were poured in, so the situation worsened. It was a vicious spiral from which there was no escape, and from which the Luftwaffe fighter arm in the west never fully recovered.

It was later estimated that 30 to 40 of these young pilots – the numerical equivalent of a complete *Gruppe* – were shot down for every experienced formation leader lost over Normandy. The crucial test was widely held to be the first six missions, for 'If a youngster could survive these, he stood a good chance of making it'. But a great number did not. Many failed to return from their first mission.

Among III./JG 54's earliest reinforcements were eight Fw 190s – out of 20 which had set off from Cologne – which put down at Villacoublay in the middle of a fighter-bomber attack on the evening of 9 June. The formation leader, Oberleutnant Wilhelm Heilmann, arrived the following morning, having first landed by mistake at nearby Buc, and was promptly given command of 7. *Staffel* to replace the wounded 'Fred' Teumer.

To boost the *Gruppe's* meagre strength, Hauptmann Weiss had been allocated a fourth *Staffel*, 2./JG 54 arriving fresh from the eastern front at the beginning of June. Almost as if to underline the difference between the two theatres, the unit immediately began to suffer a steady succession of losses. Among the casualties was *Staffelkapitän* Leutnant Horst Forbig, who was reported missing near Caen on 12 June after claiming a P-47 (his 58th kill, and sole Normandy victory).

Posing here with his two 'black men', Oberfeldwebel Schröder (left) and Feldwebel Löwe (right), Oberleutnant Alfred Teumer, the *Kapitän* of 7. *Staffel*, would be awarded the Knight's Cross on 19 August (for 76 kills). 'Fred' Teumer was posted to the Me 262-equipped *Kommando Nowotny* on 1 October, but was killed when his jet suffered an engine flame-out while on his approach to landing at Hesepe three days later

Such was the Allies' overwhelming superiority that the Luftwaffe was not even safe when on the ground. On 15 June B-24s of the Eighth Air Force mounted a series of raids on airfields west of Paris, and extensive damage was caused. At Villacoublay it was once again the luckless 7. *Staffel* which was hardest hit, virtually all of its equipment being destroyed. Units were now much safer after they had dispersed to smaller, unmade landing strips in the surrounding country-side. Nevertheless, throughout the campaign *Jagdwaffe* aircraft would continue to fall prey to roving bands of Allied fighter-bombers, which pounced upon the smallest sign of activity.

In the face of all these difficulties the *Gruppe* continued to fight on. On 21 July – with its serviceability returns still hovering stubbornly around the 15 mark, despite all the attempts at reinforcement in the interim – Hauptmann Robert Weiss was officially appointed *Kommandeur* of III./JG 54. By the end of the month, although the *Gruppe* had sustained over 50 casualties (32 pilots killed or missing, plus 19 wounded), the 'Green Hearts' in Normandy had claimed more than 90 enemy aircraft destroyed. By mid-August that total would have risen well above 100, making III./JG 54 the most successful *Jagdgruppe* on the invasion front.

The highest scoring of the *Gruppe's* pilots had been the *Kommandeur* himself with 18. Also achieving double figures were Hauptmann Emil Lang, the *Kapitän* of 9. *Staffel*, who claimed 14 before being appointed *Gruppenkommandeur* of II./JG 26 (with whom he would score a further 14!), and 8. *Staffel's* Leutnant Alfred Gross – another subsequent transferee to II./JG 26 – with 11.

But individual successes do not turn the tide of war, and during the latter half of August the survivors of III./JG 54 staged slowly back to Oldenburg, in northern Germany, via Beauvais, Florennes in Belgium and Bonn-Hangelar. It was after arrival in Oldenburg in the first week of September that the *Gruppe* was re-constituted on a four-*Staffel* basis as tabled below:

III./JG 54:   9. *Staffel* - as before
10. *Staffel* - ex-7. *Staffel*
11. *Staffel* - ex-8. *Staffel*
12. *Staffel* - ex-2. *Staffel*

Ex-infantryman turned fighter pilot Leutnant Hans Dortenmann took over as *Kapitän* of 2. *Staffel* after the loss of Leutnant Forbig. The III. *Gruppe* badge is clearly visible here, but less so 2. *Staffel's* emblem on the cowling (the devil riding a trident). Dortenmann was forced to bail out of this 'Red 1' – nicknamed *'Hascherl'* ('Poor devil') – after clashing with Spitfires over Paris on 26 June

The upright propeller and gutted cockpit area point to this – possibly unserviceable – 8. *Staffel* machine having been deliberately destroyed and abandoned during the retreat from Normandy

Hauptmann Rudolf Klemm assumed command of IV./JG 54 after its near annihilation over the Arnhem area in the latter half of September 1944. He is pictured here over two years earlier on 4 April 1942 when, as an oberfeldwebel with 8. *Staffel* in Russia, he had been credited with the *Geschwader's* 2000th victory of the war

Much of September at Oldenburg was occupied in bringing the *Gruppe* back to full strength. New pilots arrived. The majority of these, however, were not youngsters fresh from fighter school, but older men – some highly decorated – from disbanded bomber units.

Although their rank and seniority might otherwise have qualified them for command positions, their previous multi-engined experience counted for little in a frontline *Jagdgruppe*. Most, therefore, initially flew as wingmen to gain the necessary expertise on single-engined fighters. And they had a new fighter – arguably the best piston-engined machine to enter Luftwaffe service during the war – upon which to prove their worth. For III./JG 54 had been selected as the first *Jagdgruppe* to receive the latest version of the Fw 190 – the D-9, or 'Long Nose'.

While 'Bazi' Weiss's unit was busy restructuring itself – new designations, new pilots, new machines – another 'Green Heart' *Gruppe* had entered the fray against the western Allies. IV./JG 54 had been activated just over a year earlier for service on the eastern front to make up for the shortfall in numbers caused by the departure of III. *Gruppe*. It had recently suffered severely during the great Soviet summer offensive of 1944 on the central sector and had been withdrawn to Germany to refit.

Commanded by Major Wolfgang Späte, IV./JG 54 was based at Löbnitz, north of Leipzig, when Allied airborne forces landed at Arnhem on 17 September. This ambitious operation, intended to smash open a path into north-west Germany, would ultimately end in failure. But before the Allied forces retired from their 'bridge too far', the Arnhem area would witness some of the fiercest fighting of the autumn. The Luftwaffe reaction to this sudden threat is not well documented, but among the units known to have been involved was IV./JG 54, which moved up to Plantlünne, close to the German-Dutch border, 24 hours after the landings began.

The *Gruppe's* attempt at intervention against the Arnhem 'corridor' was an unmitigated disaster, its carefully rebuilt strength being simply swamped by the overwhelming numbers of Allied fighters now operating from bases on mainland Europe. In little more than a fortnight IV./JG 54 was virtually annihilated.

Beginning with 14. *Staffel's* Feldwebel Eugen Gottstein, whose Fw 190 was brought down during a low-level attack on Allied troops south of Arnhem on 19 September, the *Gruppe* suffered no fewer than 17 pilots killed or missing, plus a further 6 wounded. Twenty-seven of its fighters had been lost, written-off or damaged. On 7 October the few remaining survivors were withdrawn back to the Leipzig area, this time to Mörtitz.

Here, under the command of Hauptmann Rudolf Klemm – transferred across from III. *Gruppe* to replace Wolfgang Späte, who had returned to his operational development work on the rocket-powered Me 163 – IV./JG 54 began to re-equip from scratch again for the second time in a month!

Meanwhile, III. *Gruppe's* conversion onto D-9s at Oldenburg had been progressing relatively smoothly, if slowly, and without undue incident. Once again it was Hauptmann Robert Weiss who led the way by claiming the first kill to be achieved on the new type when he intercepted and brought down an RAF reconnaissance Spitfire south of Bremen on 28 September.

Exactly a fortnight later, on 12 October, Hauptmann Weiss 'lost' two of his *Staffeln* when 9. and 12./JG 54 were deployed to Hesepe and Achmer respectively. These two airfields, situated north north-west of Osnabrück and only some six miles (10 km) apart, had recently become home to the two *Staffeln* of the Me 262-equipped *Kommando Nowotny*.

As its name implies, this pioneering jet fighter unit was headed by JG 54's very own Walter Nowotny, whose stellar career with the 'Green Hearts' on the eastern front had seen his rise from leutnant in the *Ergänzungsgruppe* to *Kommandeur* of I. *Gruppe*. Along the way he had amassed 255 victories, which feat resulted in a ban on further operational flying. After only a few months as *Kommodore* of a training *Geschwader* (JG 101) in France, however, he was appointed leader of the jet *Kommando* which bore his name on 20 September 1944.

Although the primary function of the *Kommando* was to evaluate the Me 262 fighter under combat conditions, previous experience had already shown that the revolutionary twin-engined jet was at its most vulnerable during take-off and landing – the temperamental turbojet powerplants demanded ultra-smooth throttle control, which in turn dictated a long, gradual climb at take-off and a lengthy, shallow approach prior to landing. It was to protect Nowotny's Me 262s against the ever-present threat of marauding Allied fighters during these periods that the two *Staffeln* of IV./JG 54 'Long Noses' had been detached to share their airfields.

It was no easy task, as Oberleutnant Heilmann's 9. *Staffel* at Hesepe found to its cost just three days after arrival. In a bruising engagement with Eighth Air Force P-47s on 15 October it lost six D-9s, with four pilots killed and a fifth wounded. Nor were enemy fighters the only danger they faced. The airfields' own flak defences also posed an ever-present threat. In one 48-hour period 12. *Staffel* had three machines brought down by 'friendly' fire as they pursued intruders through anti-aircraft barrages.

In addition to the specific airfield defence duties of 9. and 12./JG 54, all four of Hauptmann Weiss' *Staffeln* – although ostensibly still under training on their 'Long Noses' – soon became caught up in general operations as Anglo-American pressure against the western front mounted. On 2 November Oberleutnant Hans Dortenmann, the *Kapitän* of 12. *Staffel*, claimed one of only two heavy bombers to be credited to the *Gruppe's* D-9s. The second fell to Feldwebel Walfried Huth during the same engagement in the Osnabrück region. The new Focke-Wulf's major strength was as an air superiority fighter. All 38 of the remaining victories claimed by III./JG 54 during its final months' campaigning would – with the exception of a single reconnaissance Mosquito – be fighters.

IV. *Gruppe*, on the other hand, having re-equipped with a fresh new complement of Fw 190A-8s and transferring to Münster-Handorf on 19 November (and thence to Vörden 48 hours later), was at last able to take its place in the Defence of the Reich organisation – a move which had been thwarted by its involvement in the Arnhem operation of mid-September.

On 26 November IV./JG 54 suffered its first casualties in its new role. One of the two pilots killed that day was the *Kapitän* of 16. *Staffel*, Leutnant Heinrich 'Bazi' Sterr, a 130-victory *Experte* and Knight's Cross wearer from the eastern front, who was bounced by a pair of P-51s while attempting to land at Vörden. Twenty-four hours later the *Gruppe* lost three more killed and one wounded. But soon the unit's activities were once again being dictated by events unfolding on the ground.

On 16 December Hitler unleashed his last great gamble in the west – the counter-offensive through the Ardennes. Operating under the control of JG 27, Hauptmann Klemm's IV./JG 54 was called upon to provide aerial cover above the battlefield and the surrounding areas, and to fly ground-attack missions in direct support of the advancing Panzers. And, as at Arnhem three months earlier, it was bled dry in the process. During the last two weeks of December 25 pilots were reported killed or missing.

The casualties included two more *Staffelkapitäne*. 'Bazi' Sterr's replacement at the head of 16./JG 54, Leutnant Paul Brandt – who, as an NCO, had been awarded the Knight's Cross on 29 September (for 30 victories), two-thirds of which had been achieved in the west – was shot down by 2nd TAF Tempests north of the 'Bulge' on 24 December. Three days later 14. *Staffel's* Leutnant Alfred Budde fell victim to P-47s over the Ardennes close to the German border.

It was also on 24 December that 9. and 12./JG 54 had returned to the III. *Gruppe* fold, leaving Hesepe and Achmer to rejoin Hauptmann Weiss' *Gruppenstab* and the other two *Staffeln* at Varrelbusch. III./JG 54 had scored no victories, and suffered no casualties, since 7 November (the day Leutnant Peter Crump, *Kapitän* of 10. *Staffel*, had claimed the reconnaissance Mosquito south-west of Oldenburg). But that was about to change.

Now reunited, on 25 December the *Gruppe* was placed under the command of Oberstleutnant Josef 'Pips' Priller's JG 26, which by this time was also operating Fw 190D-9s. On 27 December III./JG 54's 'Long Noses' clashed with a squadron of New Zealand Tempests near Münster-Handorf. Leutnant Crump was responsible for two of the three Tempests claimed (although, in fact, only one was actually destroyed). The *Gruppe* suffered three killed and two wounded. It was not an auspicious return to action. It was as nothing, however, compared to the storm which broke 48 hours later.

Once again the D-9s were pitted against RAF fighters of 2nd TAF reported in the area to the north of Münster. Although it was to be a full *Gruppe* effort, for some reason Divisional HQ had specifically ordered each *Staffel* to take off separately, at hourly intervals, and to fly at low altitude. In the face of the enemy's known numerical superiority, such piecemeal use of relatively small formations was a recipe for disaster – and a disaster is exactly what ensued.

First to set out were Oberleutnant Wilhelm Heilmann's 9. *Staffel*. Predictably enough, it was jumped by enemy fighters led by a squadron of Canadian Spitfires. Although 'Willi' Heilmann managed to belly-land his damaged machine, six of his pilots were killed.

Aware of the situation, but unwilling to disobey the strict orders from above, Hauptmann Robert Weiss took off with his *Stabsschwarm* an hour later, just ahead of Hauptmann Wilhelm Bottländer's 11. *Staffel*, in the hope of averting a complete catastrophe. Instead, both the *Gruppenkommandeur* and his wingman, Oberleutnant Ernst Bellaire, lost their lives, as too did four pilots of 11./JG 54. Although he waited the obligatory hour, Oberleutnant Hans Dortenmann, *Kapitän* of 12. *Staffel*, ignored the low level edict and thus lost just one killed and another wounded. Only Peter Crump's 10./JG 54 escaped entirely without loss.

Although the *Gruppe* had, in turn, claimed six Spitfires and two Typhoons, its thirteen dead and two wounded were the heaviest casualties III./JG 54 ever suffered in a single day. Henceforth, 29 December would always be referred to as *'der schwarze Tag'* – the 'Black Day'.

Given their recent high rates of attrition (III./JG 54 up near the Dutch border, IV./JG 54 over the Ardennes region), it is a tribute to the two *Gruppen*'s tireless groundcrews that both were able to participate in Unternehmen *Bodenplatte* (Operation *Baseplate*). This concerted attack on Allied airfields in the Low Countries by over 900 aircraft, timed for the morning of 1 January 1945, was the aerial equivalent of the Ardennes counter-offensive – a 'last throw' attempt by the *Jagdwaffe* to reverse its fortunes in the west.

Under acting *Kommandeur* Hans Dortenmann, III./JG 54's 17 serviceable Fw 190D-9s moved forward from Varrelbusch to Fürstenau. From here they would accompany some 160 fighters of JG 26 towards their assigned targets – the airfields around Brussels. III./JG 54's specific objective was Grimbergen. After a 50-minute dog-leg approach flight, which cost them their first casualty to 'friendly' flak west of Rotterdam, the *Gruppe* raced across the airfield at an altitude of little more than 650 ft (200 m) . . . and found it practically deserted!

The half-dozen or so aircraft parked between the empty hangars were a poor return for the *Gruppe*'s own losses. Nine pilots failed to return from *Bodenplatte* and another was wounded. Among the five dead was 'Willi' Bottländer, the *Kapitän* of 11. *Staffel*. Other *Gruppen* taking part in the New Year's Day attack would sustain higher casualties, but none suffered a greater proportionate loss than III./JG 54. It had sacrificed close on 60 per cent of its strength to very little purpose. The shattered *Gruppe* would not be back in action until the fourth week in January.

In comparison, Hauptmann Rudolf Klemm's IV. *Gruppe* at Vörden was able to contribute 25 Fw 190A-8s and -9s to JG 27's attack on Brussels-Melsbroek. This was more successful, with at least 11 Wellingtons and three Spitfires destroyed on the ground. The cost to IV./JG 54 was one dead, one missing and one PoW.

Despite escaping from *Bodenplatte* so lightly, it was a fortnight before IV. *Gruppe* was committed to its next major operation. This took place on 14 January, and was directed against Eighth Air Force 'heavies' attacking Osnabrück. But IV./JG 54's Focke-Wulf's were unable to penetrate the

One of the oddest of all *Bodenplatte* losses was that of 10. *Staffel's* Leutnant Theo Nibel. His 'Black 12' was reportedly brought down by a bird strike, for as the Fw 190D-9 roared low over Grimbergen, a rising pheasant damaged its radiator. The fate of the hapless fowl has gone unrecorded, but the 'Long Nose' ended up on its belly near the village of Wemmel, and Leutnant Nibel was taken prisoner

Oberleutnant Hans Dortenmann, the *Staffelkapitän* of 12./JG 54 (centre), and four extremely youthful looking NCO pilots of 11. and 12. *Staffeln* stroll through the snow at Varrelbusch in early February 1945. All would survive the final three months of the war, with the exception of Unteroffizier Werner Merz (far left), who fell victim to P-51s on 18 March (after III./JG 54's redesignation as IV./JG 26)

bombers' P-51 fighter screen and lost eight killed, including two *Staffelkapitäne*, and two wounded. It was the final blow.

This time there was no reprieve for the *Gruppe* which, on three previous occasions, had risen phoenix-like from near total annihilation – in Russia, at Arnhem and over the Ardennes. After moving to Gardelegen IV./JG 54 was redesignated as II./JG 7 on 12 February. Command passed to Major Hermann Staiger, who was to oversee conversion onto the Me 262 jet. The process was never completed.

III./JG 54 would remain in existence for another fortnight. The *Gruppe* had resumed its personal war against 2nd TAF on 23 January 1945, losing eight D-9s (four pilots killed) over north-west Germany but being credited with one Tempest and a pair of Spitfires in return. A change of location and opposition brought better results on 13 February when, at a cost of two dead, III./JG 54 claimed at least eight Ninth Air Force P-47s flying armed reconnaissance sweeps over the Montabaur area east of Koblenz.

The following day acting *Kommandeur* Oberleutnant 'Willi' Heilmann was replaced by Major Rudolf Klemm (ex-IV. *Gruppe*). On 21 February III./JG 54's pilots downed a trio each of P-47s and P-51s for the loss of one of their pilots. But it was against the 2nd TAF that their last combat took place. On 24 February 10. *Staffel's* Feldwebel Erich Lange was killed in action against Tempests, and 9. *Staffel's* Unteroffizier Brisch shot down a Canadian-flown Spitfire, both in the Rheine area.

Twenty-four hours later III./JG 54 was officially redesignated as IV./JG 26.

At the end of February 1945 a 'second' III./JG 54 was created by redesignating II./ZG 76, a twin-engined *Zerstörergruppe.* Based at Grossenhain, north of Dresden, under Hauptmann Karl-Fritz Schloßstein, this *Gruppe* was converted from its Me 410s onto the Fw 190. Although inspected at Grossenhain by Major Dietrich Hrabak, the *Kommodore* of JG 54, the new unit never came under the *Geschwader's* direct control. After transferring to Eggersdorf, east of Berlin, its operational orders emanated directly from local *Jagddivision* HQ at nearby Bad Saarow.

After losing its first Fw 190A-8 to ground fire on 9 March, and two more to enemy action 48 hours later, the inexperienced III./JG 54 was caught taking off from Eggersdorf on 22 March by P-51s of the Eighth Air Force's veteran 4th FG. Six of the Focke-Wulfs were shot down, five being claimed by the Deputy Group Commander, Lt Col S S Woods. The following day another half-dozen Fw 190s were damaged when their field was ground-strafed. Early in April the decimated *Gruppe* was disbanded.

Although the story of the 'Green Hearts' in the west had ended not with a bang, but with something of a confused whimper amidst a welter of redesignations, the two eastern front *Gruppen* would fight stoically on until the very end.

EASTERN FRONT 1943-45

On 6 July 1943, the second day of the Kursk offensive, Hannes Trautloft – having been in office for almost three years – had handed over command of JG 54 to Major Hubertus von Bonin. The latter was no stranger to the *Geschwader*. Earlier in the war he had been *Kommandeur* of I./JG 54 for more than 18 months prior to his transfer to JG 52.

Now returned as *Kommodore*, von Bonin was to oversee a new, more fluid phase in JG 54's war against the Soviets as, in the aftermath of '*Zitadelle*', his fighters were first used even more extensively as a 'fire brigade', shuttling from one fresh area of danger to another along all three main sectors of the eastern front, before their final lengthy entrenchment back up along the shores of the Baltic.

To recompense for the non-return of III./JG 54 from the west, von Bonin had been given a new *Gruppe* to add to his line-up in Russia. IV./JG 54 was activated from scratch on Bf 109Gs at Jesau in East Prussia (the original home of III. *Gruppe*) during July 1943. It was headed by Hauptmann Erich Rudorffer, a 74-victory *Experte* and Knight's Cross wearer from JG 2.

On 22 July, while IV. *Gruppe* was still busy working-up, yet another Soviet offensive was launched against the Leningrad front. Its objective was to push German forces even farther back from the city. As the only Luftwaffe fighters in the area, *Stab* and II./JG 54's 30+ serviceable Fw 190s were heavily committed. While its Focke-Wulfs were facing the Red Air Force in the skies overhead, II. *Gruppe* also deployed a handful of Bf 109G-2s on ground-attack sorties against the Soviet army.

These missions were not at all popular with the pilots involved. They reportedly had an arrangement between themselves whereby a bottle of champagne was awarded to anyone who 'inadvertently' managed to write-off one of the Messerschmitts in a heavy landing!

As well as the Messerschmitts of II. *Gruppe*, there was also a dedicated fighter-bomber *Staffel* of Fw 190s in action alongside them on the northern sector. This dozen-strong unit operated under the designation 12./JG 54, for the 10. and 11./JG 54 slots had already been taken by the western-based *Jabo* and high-altitude *Staffeln* respectively.

On 30 July Hauptmann Heinrich Jung, *Kommandeur* of II. *Gruppe*,

By the summer of 1943 on the eastern front, JG 54's unit badges were a thing of the past. An official edict had banned all such distinguishing emblems in order to make it more difficult for the Soviets to keep track of unit movements. Patches of overspray on the cowling and beneath the cockpit of 'Black 7' – reportedly the mount of 5. *Staffel's* Leutnant Emil Lang (see colour profile 25) – indicate where the 'Lion of Aspern' and the 'Green Heart' had once been on proud display was lost during a dogfight over the forests east of Mga. Jung had claimed a Soviet La-5, his 68th and final victory, before being shot down himself. He would be awarded a posthumous Knight's Cross on 12 November. Command of II./JG 54 passed to Hauptmann Erich Rudorffer, whose IV. *Gruppe* were nearing the completion of its training in the Reich. Jung's death and Rudorffer's sudden departure left IV./JG 54 temporarily leaderless. It was not until after the *Gruppe* had moved up to Siverskaya in August to reinforce II./JG 54 on the Leningrad front that a new *Kommandeur* arrived in the person of Hauptmann Rudolf Sinner, latterly *Gruppenkommandeur* of IV./JG 27 in the Aegean theatre.

Meanwhile, I./JG 54, which had remained under *Luftflotte* 6 on the central sector after the premature abandonment of 'Zitadelle', had been suffering losses too. On 3 August Major Gerhard Homuth, another ex-Mediterranean *Experte* from JG 27, who had been brought in to head the *Gruppe* after 'Seppl' Seiler's wounding on day two of the Kursk offensive, failed to return from his second mission as *Gruppenkommandeur*.

Oberleutnant Hans Götz, *Staffelkapitän* of 2./JG 54, immediately stepped into the breach as acting *Kommandeur*, only to be lost on the very next day. His 'Black 2' was last sighted going down inverted into the forested region east of Bryansk after an unsuccessful attack on a formation of heavily-armoured Il-2 *Sturmoviks*.

Twenty-four hours later, on 5 August, the Red Army recaptured Orel. I./JG 54 retired westwards to Ivanovka. Soviet pressure was increasing all along the central sector, and on 18 August the Russians mounted another heavy attack in the area to the south of Lake Ilmen, forcing II. and IV./JG 54 to divert their attention away from the Leningrad fighting to help counter this latest threat along the boundary between Army Groups' North and Centre to their rear. Not surprisingly, the casualty lists of all three *Gruppen* began to lengthen.

On 19 August II. *Gruppe* lost one of its old guard when Oberleutnant Max Stotz finally met his match during an encounter with a large formation of Yak fighters near Vitebsk, just across the boundary on the central sector. Although Stotz's stricken Fw 190 was seen to crash and explode on impact, he had apparently managed to take to his parachute. He was spotted drifting down over enemy-held territory, but thereafter disappeared without trace. Having risen to the position of *Staffelkapitän* of 5./JG 54, Stotz's final total of 189 victories puts him among the top 20 highest-scoring Luftwaffe *Experten* of the war.

It was against this unlikely background of mounting attrition, and the beginnings of the general retreat, that an even more successful 'Green Heart' pilot was to reach the pinnacle of his career. I./JG 54's loss of three leaders in quick succession – Seiler, Homuth and Götz – had undoubtedly been a blow for the *Gruppe*. But their fourth *Kommandeur* in the space of little more than six weeks was to prove not just longer lasting, but inspirational.

On 13 August Oberleutnant Walter Nowotny, *Staffelkapitän* of 1./JG 54, had claimed nine kills to bring his total to 137. Five days later he reached the 150 mark. Three days after that – on 21 August, when another seven victories raised his overall tally to 161 – Walter Nowotny was appointed *Gruppenkommandeur* of I./JG 54. In a letter written the following day Nowotny described his reaction to the news;

Oberleutnant Hans Götz, *StaKa* of 2./JG 54, was lost on only his second day as acting *Kommandeur* of I. *Gruppe* when he was shot down near Bryansk on 4 May 1943

Another August loss was that of Hauptmann Max Stotz, *StaKa* of 5./JG 54, who had first joined the Austrian air arm in 1935, and had served with the Aspern *Gruppe* since before the outbreak of war. This picture was taken in 1942, prior to Oberfeldwebel Stotz's winning the Oak Leaves

'Got my 161st yesterday, in other words 37 in ten days. Also informed I was to be the new *Kommandeur*. Two happy events that we celebrated accordingly! It's not every day that a 22^1/$_2$-year-old gets made up to *Kommandeur* – that's normally a Major's post, which means that sooner or later I'll get to be a Hauptmann, or perhaps even a Major. Something I'd never dreamed of. Still no sign of the Oak Leaves though.'

The touch of pique revealed in the closing sentence of this missive was understandable. Just as in the case of his belated Knight's Cross so, Nowotny felt, the Oak Leaves were long overdue. Others had received the award for far fewer victories than Nowotny had currently amassed.

The first such decorations of the war had been won with just 40 kills. In the three years since, however, this numerical yardstick had been progressively added to – particularly on the eastern front, where the numbers of enemy aircraft shot down had exceeded all expectations. Yet despite a complicated points system for specific types of aerial victories, wide discrepancies still remained between individual awards. Other factors, such as leadership, obviously came into the equation. But Walter Nowotny could not be faulted on this score.

In fact, there were no sinister overtones in the withholding of Nowotny's rightful honours. He had simply been unfortunate. Each time he had neared the requisite number of kills for a particular decoration, the goal posts had suddenly been moved. In the case of the Oak Leaves, the 120 victories which would have ensured this prestigious decoration earlier in the year had now been upped by another 70 or so.

Nowotny was not the only one to fall victim to this arbitrary numbers trap. But it made him all the more determined. His reply to a letter from his oldest brother, enquiring whether he might have upset the powers-that-be in some way, was terse. It was, he informed Rudolf, 'none of your business' and besides, 'if "they" don't want to give me the Oak Leaves, I'll get myself the Diamonds'. And in just over six weeks he would do just that!

In August Walter Nowotny had claimed a total of 49 kills. But during the same period the three eastern front *Gruppen* had suffered 18 pilots killed or missing, plus a further six wounded. While this rate of loss might not seem extortionate, it represented close on a third of the unit's current operational strength. By the end of the month Major von Bonin's *Geschwaderstab* had joined Nowotny's I. *Gruppe* on the central sector while II. and IV./JG 54 continued to shuttle back and forth from the northern fields of Krasnogvardeisk, Siverskaya and Mga to the area around Vitebsk, on the central front, as the situation demanded.

And the situation was deteriorating – everywhere. A determined Soviet offensive in the south had recaptured Kharkov, one of the strongest German bastions in the Ukraine, on 23 August. Now the Red Army was approaching the River Dnieper and beginning to threaten the Ukrainian capital Kiev. In September the 'Green Hearts' became even more thinly stretched, as for the first time they found themselves operating over all three sectors simultaneously as Soviet pressure increased along the entire length of the eastern front.

In the north the two-dozen serviceable *Gustavs* of Hauptmann Sinner's IV./JG 54 remained under the control of *Luftflotte* 1 as sole guardians of the Leningrad front. In the centre the *Stab* and I. *Gruppe's* combined strength of 20 Fw 190s continued to serve under *Luftflotte* 6, facing the

Hauptman Walter Nowotny, recently appointed *Gruppenkommandeur* of I./JG 54, awaits at the end of the line (furthest from the camera) to be presented with both the Oak Leaves and the Swords from the hands of the Führer on 22 September 1943. The others recipients are, from the left, Major Hartmann Grasser (JG 51, Oak Leaves), Hauptmann Heinrich Prinz von Sayn-Wittgenstein (NJG 3, Oak Leaves) and Hauptmann Günther Rall (JG 52, Swords)

Soviet advance westward from Kursk. Meanwhile, Hauptmann Rudorffer's II./JG 54, also some 20 Focke-Wulfs strong, had been despatched to Kiev, in the southern sector, to reinforce *Luftflotte* 4's 'resident' fighters – the Bf 109s of JG 52 – in an attempt to stem the Red Army's drive across the Ukraine.

In the month of September, Nowotny's rise was meteoric. On the 1st of the month he claimed ten kills (the second time in his career that he had been credited with ten in one day), which took his overall tally to 183. Seventy-two hours later that figure had risen to 189, and Walter Nowotny finally won his long-awaited Oak Leaves. Eleven more victories over the next four days gave him his double century on 8 September. And exactly one week later, on 15 September, Nowotny's total of 215 made him the then highest-scoring pilot in the entire Luftwaffe.

The last 12 of Nowotny's victories had been claimed during the previous two days while defending the *Gruppe's* own airfield. The base at Shatalovka-East had recently been subject to heavy Soviet air attack, and four German fighters had been destroyed and as many again damaged. Two pilots, both from the attached 12. *Jabostaffel*, had been killed and Oberleutnant 'Bazi' Weiss, the *Kapitän* of 3./JG 54, was wounded.

Nowotny had already been instructed to attend Adolf Hitler's *'Wolfs-chanze'* ('Wolf's Lair') HQ in East Prussia to be presented with his Oak Leaves, but before doing so, he was to claim three further kills – a brace of La-5s and a Yak-9 shot down out of a gaggle of 20+ fighters encountered near Yelnya on 17 September. Those same 'powers-that-be' who had been so dilatory in the past more than made up for it now. This latest trio of victories immediately earned Oberleutnant Walter Nowotny his Swords. Five days later he received both awards from the hands of the Führer.

And still Nowotny's star – and his score – continued to rise. On 1 October he was promoted to hauptmann. A week later four kills in the space of as many minutes saw his total climb to 223. One of his eight claims of 9 October gave JG 54 its 6000th victory of the war, and on 11 October he claimed four yet again, although this time they took nine minutes to despatch. And nine more kills over the next 48 hours left him just six short of 250.

Although Hauptmann Walter Nowotny has obeyed the rules concerning the display of unit badges, he still retains his personal 'Lucky 13' . . .

Those six – a pair each of LaGG-3s, La-5s and P-40s – fell on the following day. On 14 October Hauptmann Walter Nowotny had become the first fighter pilot in the world to score 250 victories! Five days later he was back at the *'Wolfsschanze'*, this time to be awarded the Diamonds. He was only the eighth member of all the armed forces to be so honoured – and the sixth of just seven *Jagdwaffe* pilots to receive the Diamonds during the course of the war.

Although it was Nowotny who was fêted by the Goebbel's propaganda machine, he himself was the first to admit that his extraordinary run of success would never have been achieved without the unstinting support of others, both on the ground and in the air. Foremost among the latter was his long-serving wingman, and great friend, Karl 'Quax' Schnörrer. Two others who regularly flew with Nowotny were Anton 'Toni' Döbele and Rudolf Rademacher. This quartet made a formidable team.

As the 'Nowotny *Schwarm*' they were famous throughout the eastern theatre. And rightly so, for between them they would be responsible for the destruction of 474 Soviet aircraft .

One member of II. *Gruppe* in the south was also about to become a national celebrity. Since transferring to Kiev-West on 20 September, II./JG 54 had been engaged primarily in flying *Freie Jagd* sweeps. Its principle role was to protect the retreating ground troops from the attentions of the ubiquitous *Sturmoviks*, and this it did throughout October. But two-dozen Focke-Wulfs cannot stop an army, and by the end of the month Soviet forces were threatening the Ukrainian capital from both flanks.

II./JG 54 was ordered to withdraw to Belaya Zerkov, some 46 miles (75 km) south south-east of Kiev. But a single *Schwarm* was instructed to provide 'direct support for the army troops fighting in Kiev for as long as possible'. Leutnant Emil Lang, *Staffelkapitän* of 5./JG 54, called for volunteers. Every pilot's hand went up. Lang selected his *Schwarm* members, plus one reserve, and the remainder of the *Gruppe* duly departed. The small *Kommando*, consisting of five Fw 190s, plus eight groundcrew, three trucks and a tanker, were left alone on the deserted airfield.

Concealing the five fighters and three of the vehicles in a corner of one of the empty hangars, the party drove to a barracks block on the outskirts of town to spend a night punctuated by nearby machine-gun and small arms fire. Leutnant Norbert Hannig takes up the story;

'At first light on 3 November we drove back to the airfield. We had hardly arrived when all hell broke loose. The Soviet assault on Kiev opened with artillery barrages from both north and south, together with a mass of bombers and ground-attack aircraft supported by hordes of La-5 and Yak-7 fighters. Wherever you looked Soviet aircraft filled the sky, undisturbed by German flak or fighters.

'In one of the few quiet moments Leutnant Lang took off with Unteroffizier Paschke as his wingman. They disappeared off to the west. The second *Rotte* was to remain on the ground until their return. Wave after wave of Soviets were coming in, dropping their bombs on the German positions ringing the city and then immediately turning back eastwards.

'Suddenly, two Fw 190s appeared high out of the east and dived on a bunch of fighters escorting a formation of Il-2s. A short burst of fire, an La-5 is hit, catches fire, dives vertically trailing a banner of smoke and

. . . which is more clearly visible here as he vaults from the cockpit of his Fw 190. It was in this machine that he claimed his 250th kill on 14 October 1943 – and thereby became the only member of JG 54 to be awarded the Diamonds

Portrait of a national hero – Hauptmann Walter Nowotny . . .

... and the trio who, along with their illustrious leader, made up the famous 'Nowotny *Schwarm*'. From the left, Oberfeldwebel Anton 'Toni' Döbele, Unteroffizier Karl 'Quax' Schnörrer and Oberfeldwebel Rudolf 'Rudi' Rademacher

Pictures of indifferent quality – taken from a wartime German newsreel – but of some historic significance as Leutnant Emil Lang claims a world-record 18 victories in a single day! Lang and Unteroffizier Paschke return from the first of the day's four sorties ...

explodes into the ground to the north of us. The Fw 190 slides into a left-hand turn beneath one of the Il-2s, a line of tracer, another hit . . . and the second Soviet goes down. Soon the untidy formation of *Sturmoviks* is out of sight. Russian fighters hover overhead. We wait.

'After about an hour "Bully" Lang returns. Taxying up to the hangar, he yells "Stoppages in both right-hand cannon. Get the reserve machine ready. Gross, you'll be my wingman". He hurriedly changes aircraft, and soon he and Unteroffizier Gross are off and the whole *Zirkus* starts all over again.

'Meanwhile, Paschke is describing the first sortie. Lang had scored four kills. In this second he got six. During the third, again with Gross on his wing, he claimed a further five. For the fourth sortie of the day it was the turn of Feldwebel Hoffmann to fly as wingman. Lang was now just three short of his century, and "Lerge" Hoffmann two away from his fifty.

'It was afternoon by this time, but still the waves of Soviet bombers kept on coming, with Bostons joining the Il-2s. Lang landed about an hour later with the three required victories under his belt, and he was carried shoulder-high from his fighter by the jubilant mechanics. Shortly afterwards Hoffmann returned safely. He too had scored his double . . . "Congratulations on your 50th, Hoffmann!" . . . "Danke, Herr Leutnant, and my congratulations on your hundredth!"

'On the way back to the hangar, still fired up by the day's fighting, Leutnant Lang described his final kill, " . . . and when he saw me on his tail, instead of breaking away the idiot performed a roll. I pressed the trigger and his starboard wing sheared off. He jumped out and hung there in his parachute. That was the hundredth".'

It was the culmination of an amazing three weeks for 'Bully' Lang. During that time the ex-Lufthansa pilot had claimed no fewer than 72 victories around Kiev – a dozen on 21 October alone. But on that 3 November, with 18 victories in a single day, Emil Lang had set an all-time world record. The feat was given wide coverage in the German media.

Photographs of Leutnant Lang on the shoulders of his groundcrew appeared on the covers of magazines (see *Osprey Aircraft of the Aces 6*, page 72), and the day's events, captured by an amateur cameraman, were shown on the weekly newsreels in cinemas throughout the Reich. What the German public did not get to hear about was what happened next.

Pilots and groundcrew returned to the abandoned barracks to spend a second night. And this time their rest was disturbed not by the sound of small arms fire, but by half a dozen T-34 tanks pulling up outside the gates!

... the fourth and final mission has been flown. 'Bully' Lang punches the air in delight – an unequalled 18 kills have given him his century. On the right, Leutnant Norbert Hannig, who was reserve pilot that day ...

While the tanks pumped round after round of cannon fire into the blazing buildings nearby, and empty shell cases clattered on to the pavement below, their searchlights played over the face of the barracks block alongside them. Accompanying Red infantrymen searched the ground floor rooms, kicking in doors and smashing furniture, but failed to spot the five German pilots crouching at the top of the stairs armed with just a single sub-machine gun, their pistols and one hand-grenade apiece.

Finally, the Soviet soldiers climbed back aboard the tanks and they moved off. At first light the five woke the mechanics (who had slept through the entire fracas!) and the group managed to make their way back to the airfield. Here, all had been relatively quiet during the night. The Focke-Wulfs took off for the temporary haven of Belaya Zerkov, where the ground party also arrived late that same evening.

Kiev was finally recaptured by the Red Army on 6 November. It was on this date that Hauptmann Erich Rudorffer, the *Kommandeur* of II. *Gruppe*, claimed 11 victories. Such individual successes were but a drop in the ocean, however, when measured against an enemy in the air whose overall strength was approaching the order of 10,000 machines! The introduction of new types and new tactics by the Soviets were also beginning to make themselves felt;

'The old days of our qualitative superiority, when it was simply a case of piling straight into a dogfight with a shout of *"Hussassa!"* (the traditional battle-cry of the Hussars), were over. By the end of 1943 it was more a matter of fighting for survival – gain the advantage of height, make one diving pass, and then get back upstairs as quickly as possible ... what we called "yo-yo" tactics.'

On the ground, too, German forces were buckling under the relentless Soviet pressure. To the north the latest offensive by the Red Army had taken the enemy to within less than 70 miles (112 km) of the Latvian border. Army Group North, already denuded of 13 divisions to help prop up the other sectors, faced the very real danger of being cut off along the Baltic coastal strip.

... the last member of the *Schwarm* returns safely. Leutnant Lang and Feldwebel Hoffmann exchange congratulations as the other members of the small *Kommando* look on. Kiev-West, 3 November 1943

In the centre, *Stab* and I./JG 54 were still experiencing mixed fortunes. On 29 October Oberfeldwebel Otto Kittel, the quiet NCO who would ultimately emerge as the 'Green Heart's' highest scorer, had been awarded the Knight's Cross for 123 kills. But the days of the famed 'Nowotny *Schwarm*' were drawing to a close. On 11 November Oberfeldwebel Anton Döbele was killed in a mid-air collision – some sources say with another Luftwaffe fighter, others with a Soviet Il-2 – over the Smolensk-Vitebsk supply highway. With his score standing just six short of a century at the time of his death, 'Toni' Döbele was posthumously commissioned and honoured with the Knight's Cross on 26 March 1944.

Twenty-four hours after Döbele's loss another member of the *Schwarm* was seriously wounded. Despite atrocious weather conditions, Feldwebel Karl Schnörrer had taken off from Vitebsk with *Gruppenkommandeur* Walter Nowotny in answer to a call for help from an infantry unit under attack by Sturmoviks. Each had managed to down an Il-2 when Nowotny realised that his wingman was on fire (Schnörrer's 'Green 2' had reportedly been hit by 'friendly' flak).

Obeying his leader's injunction to jump, 'Quax' Schnörrer bailed out of his blazing machine. But from an altitude of less than 230 ft (70 m) his parachute had insufficient time to deploy properly and Schnörrer fell heavily into a stand of trees, suffering severe concussion and breaking both legs.

On 15 November Hauptmann Walter Nowotny claimed his last two kills on the eastern front. He had scored 255 victories since joining the 'Green Hearts' (plus, according to some sources, at least another 20 unconfirmed) and was now ordered to cease operational flying. He would, however, remain at the head of I./JG 54 for another three months before assuming command of a training *Geschwader* (JG 101) in February 1944. The following autumn he established the Me 262-equipped jet fighter *Kommando* which bore his name, and which ultimately led to his death on 8 November 1944 (see *Osprey Aircraft of the Aces 17*).

Towards the close of 1943 another four Knight's Crosses were awarded to JG 54. 22 November's two recipients were both members of II. *Gruppe*: Hauptmann Emil Lang, *Kapitän* of 5. *Staffel*, for his 119 victories, and 6. *Staffel*'s Oberfeldwebel Albin Wolf for his 117. It is not quite certain exactly how many kills Albin Wolf's good friend and *Staffel* comrade Oberfeldwebel Heinrich 'Bazi' Sterr had been credited with at the time of his receiving the Knight's Cross on 5 December. But his score must have been similar to those above, for he had reportedly achieved his century the previous month.

The second of 5 December's two awards was posthumous. Leutnant Günther Scheel had joined I./JG 54 in the spring of 1943. He quickly established himself as a first-class fighter pilot, rarely returning from a mission without scoring. But his promising career had been cut short at the close of the Kursk offensive. On 16 July, while escorting a *Gruppe* of Ju 87s, he was rammed at low-level by a Yak-9 and crashed to his death behind enemy lines near Orel.

Oberfeldwebel Otto Kittel (left) is awarded the Knight's Cross, for 123 kills, at Vitesbk on 29 October. The central figure is Oberst Franz Reuss from IV. *Fliegerkorps* staff, who is talking to none other than Hauptmann Walter Nowotny

The end of the 'Nowotny *Schwarm*' came with the death of Oberfeldwebel Anton Döbele, who lost his life when his 'White 11' was involved in a mid-air collision over the Smolensk-Vitebsk highway on 11 November 1943

Pictured here as a hauptmann, Anton Mader, who had been an original member of the pre-war I./JG 76, returned to the *Geschwader* as its fourth – and penultimate – *Kommodore* on 28 January 1944 . . .

. . . and one week later, on 4 February, Hauptmann Horst Ademeit (in cap) took over from Walter Nowotny as *Kommandeur* of I. *Gruppe*

On 15 December the 'Green Hearts' lost their only *Kommodore* to be killed in action when Major Hubertus von Bonin was shot down near Vitebsk, on the southern flank of the renewed Soviet drive towards Latvia, which was now less than 40 miles (65 km) away. With their base in imminent danger of encirclement, *Stab* and I./JG 54 retired from Vitebsk to Orscha before the year was out.

In the southern sector, too, the Red Army's rapid advance westwards from Kiev forced II. *Gruppe's* withdrawal from Belaya Zerkov, and on Christmas Day it was ordered to transfer immediately to Tarnopol, in Poland. But thick fog delayed the departure for three long days while retreating army units flooded west past their airfield. A marginal improvement in the weather finally allowed the most experienced pilots to take off on 28 December, while the remainder accompanied the ground column. Staging via Vinnitsa, and only after great difficulties and no few losses, the *Gruppe* was reunited at Tarnopol in the first week of January.

Having retired out of immediate harm's way of the rampaging Red Army, JG 54 was able to pause and draw breath. The reduction in activity at the beginning of 1944 – due in no small part to that perennial Russian adversary, 'General Winter' – was demonstrated not only by the fact that Walter Nowotny still remained as titular head of I. *Gruppe* in a non-operational capacity, but also that no immediate replacement was provided for the fallen *Kommodore* Hubertus von Bonin.

Despite the all-pervading fog and heavy falls of snow, operations did not cease altogether, of course. One of the first losses of the new year was 2. *Staffel's* Oberleutnant Otto Vinzent, who had often led the *Gruppe* in the air following Nowotny's official grounding, and who was reported missing on 4 January. And ten days later I./JG 54 was able to claim 30 enemy aircraft shot down, the majority of them Il-2s supporting a localised tank attack near Orscha.

For the past two-and-a-half years the position around Leningrad had, by eastern front standards, remained remarkably static. Some had even likened the trench systems in the area to those of World War 1. But in the third week of January 1944 all that changed. A renewed Soviet offensive between Lakes Ladoga and Ilmen broke through the German lines. Mga was recaptured on 21 January and the Red Army pushed south-westwards towards Krasnogvardeisk. With rail transport now able to move freely in and out of the city, the end of the siege of Leningrad was officially announced on 27 January.

The following day JG 54 welcomed a new *Kommodore* in the person of Oberstleutnant Anton Mader. He was another with a long-standing connection to the *Geschwader*, having been 3./JG 76's first *Staffelkapitän* back in 1938. Since decorated with the Knight's Cross, and with 68 victories to his credit, Anton Mader had latterly served as *Kommodore* of JG 11 in Defence of the Reich.

Exactly one week after Mader's arrival at Orscha, Walter Nowotny passed command of his I. *Gruppe* to Hauptmann Horst Ademeit, whose entire career had been spent with JG 54 since first joining as an NCO in 1940.

One final change of command during this period occurred on 11 February with an exchange of posts between Hauptleute Siegfried Schnell and Rudolf Sinner, the *Kommandeure* of III. and IV. *Gruppen* respectively. The reason for this individual east/west swap is not altogether clear, but the move to Russia was to prove fatal for 'Wumm' Schnell. On 25 February, just two weeks after assuming command of IV./JG 54 at Pleskau, the now Major Siegfried Schnell, who had been one of the Channel front's leading *Experten*, was killed in action against Soviet fighters over Narva.

The location of Schnell's loss illustrates just how far the troops of Army Group North had withdrawn since being driven out of their positions around Leningrad. By the end of February they were occupying the northernmost stretch of the *Panther-Stellung* (the 'Panther-position', the eastern front's equivalent of the *Westwall*), a prepared line of defences extending along the 30-mile (50 km) course of the River Narva from Lake Peipus up to the Baltic Sea.

It was over this very territory that 18. *Armee* had advanced out of Estonia in the late summer of 1941 during its coastal march on Leningrad. Now both the 18. and its sister *Armee*, the 16., deployed to the south of Lake Peipus, were being forced to retrace their steps as Soviet pressure pushed them off Russian soil and back into the Baltic states. And, to complete the circle, I. and II./JG 54 were also returned to their eastern front 'roots' by being transferred back up to the northern sector to provide aerial support for the two *Armeen* throughout the coming months of the final retreat, just as they had done during the heady days of the 1941 advance.

Stab and I. *Gruppe* had moved up to Dorpat and Wesenberg, in Estonia, before the end of February. Hauptmann Rudorffer's II. *Gruppe* followed them up to Petseri (and Dorpat) in March. This added some 45 serviceable Fw 190s to the 20+ Bf 109Gs of IV./JG 54, which had been the sole fighter presence on the northern sector of late. And such was the parlous state of the whole front in the east by this stage of the war that even the latter *Gruppe* had been relieved of a third of its reduced strength by the recent temporary transfer of 12. *Staffel* to Uman, in the Ukraine.

March 1944 was topped and tailed by a further clutch of awards for the 'Green Hearts'. On 2 March Hauptmann Ademeit received the Oak Leaves for some 120 victories (since Nowotny's 189 six months earlier, it seems the criteria for the Oak Leaves had undergone further revision!). The same day saw 'Seppl' Seiler similarly decorated for the century he had scored before being wounded at the outset of '*Zitadelle*'.

On 26 March Oberleutnant Robert 'Bazi' Weiss and Oberfeldwebel Wilhelm Philipp were each awarded the Knight's Cross (for 70 and 61). Currently members of I. *Gruppe*, both had previously served with JG 26 in the west, and both would later be victims of III./JG 54's 'Blackest Day' over the Reich. Finally, on 28 March, Oberfeldwebel Fritz Tegtmeier, whose first kill had been achieved on the opening day of *Barbarossa*, received the Knight's Cross with his score just one short of a century.

Among the 223 victims claimed by the three *Gruppen* during March, mostly above the bitter fighting currently being waged to the south of Lake Pleskau, Oberleutnant Albin Wolf's 135th, achieved on 23 March, was also the *Geschwader's* 7000th of the war. Wolf himself would add just nine more to his personal score before being killed by a direct hit from an anti-aircraft shell over Pleskau on 2 April. He would be honoured with posthumous Oak Leaves on 27 April.

By this time 2. *Staffel's* 'Quiet NCO' was in full stride. Belying his unpromising start, on 8 April the recently commissioned Leutnant Otto

Operating out of Petseri (Petschur), south of Lake Pleskau, Oberleutnant Albin Wolf, *StaKa* of 6./JG 54, claimed his 136th kill on 23 March 1944 – and gave the *Geschwader* its 7000th victory since the outbreak of hostilities

Kittel had racked up number 150. Six days and two kills later Otto Kittel was awarded the Oak Leaves. In the interim, on 11 April, Emil Lang and Erich Rudorffer had received the same decoration, for 144 and 130 respectively.

Since Siegfried Schnell's loss back in February, IV. *Gruppe's Gustavs* had been led by acting-*Kommandeur* Hauptmann Gerhard Koall. During April further elements of IV./JG 54 had been despatched, via Lemberg (Lvov) in Poland, to *Luftflotte* 4 in the far south for a brief, but disastrous, deployment alongside JG 52 in Rumania. They reportedly arrived in Mamaia with just five serviceable Bf 109s! Now, in May, Koall was appointed *Kommodore* of *Ergänzungsjagdgeschwader* 1 (EJG 1, the premier Reich-based operational fighter training unit), and the command of IV./JG 54 passed to Major Wolfgang Späte.

One of Späte's first tasks was to take his *Gruppe* back to Illesheim early in June, and there organise its conversion on to Fw 190A-8s. It was during this re-equipment that, on 22 June (the third anniversary of *Barbarossa*), the Soviets launched their great summer offensive against the central sector. As soon as it was declared operational with its new machines, IV./JG 54 was rushed forward to Lublin, in Poland, to face the full weight of the advancing Russians. It suffered swingeing losses, with nearly half its numbers killed or wounded. The casualties included *Gruppenkommandeur* Wolfgang Späte, who was injured and forced to take to his parachute, and all three of his *Staffelkapitäne*, two of whom were killed.

The survivors were withdrawn to Deblin and thence to Nasielsk, north of Warsaw. Their numbers had just been made good again, and the *Gruppe* restructured on a four-*Staffel* basis (for details see page 111) when Allied airborne troops landed at Arnhem, in Holland. Once more IV./JG 54, on paper an intact and fully re-equipped *Gruppe*, was fated to form part of a Luftwaffe response to a sudden enemy threat. But its numbers now included an even greater proportion of untried and inexperienced young pilots.

And in the west they would be opposed by the overwhelming might of Anglo-American air power. The outcome was inevitable. For the second time in a matter of weeks Späte's *Gruppe* was all but wiped out. Another withdrawal from the front and yet further replacements would be required before IV./JG 54 could resume operations against the western Allies.

All of which just left *Stab*, I. and II. *Gruppen* on their old Baltic stamping rounds. Here, too, enemy pressure was building inexorably. Throughout May the Soviets had been bombing targets in Estonia and Latvia as part of an obvious softening-up process for another offensive. JG 54's 60+ operational Fw 190s were now facing an estimated 3500 aircraft of the combined Soviet Air and Naval Air Forces on the northern sector. Despite these odds the unit claimed 83 enemy machines destroyed during the month against the loss of just four pilots.

On 16 June 1944 25 Fw 190s of 4. and 5./JG 54 were transferred to Immola, in Finland, as the fighter element of the *Gefechtsverband* Kuhlmey. Groundcrew check the engine and tune the radio of 'White 20' as part of the *Gefechtsverband's* main striking force, Ju 87s of I./SG 3, fly overhead in a ragged formation

'White 9' climbs steeply away from Immola on the afternoon of 2 July. A few hours later the Soviets mounted a heavy raid on the field, and this aircraft was destroyed when struck by a falling bomb as Unteroffizier Jakob Assmann attempted to scramble. The pilot was very fortunate to escape with only minor injuries. Altogether, the two *Staffeln* lost three Fw 190s, plus another 11 badly damaged, in the attack

But Russian activity was not directed solely westwards into the Baltic states. With Leningrad finally freed, the Red Army turned its attention to the Finnish line across the Karelian Isthmus, some 18 miles (30 km) to the north of the city. A strong attack against these positions was launched on 9 June. Forced to retreat, the Finns called upon their German allies for help.

Exactly a week later, on 16 June, a hastily assembled battle group, the *Gefechtsverband* Kuhlmey, arrived at Immola, via Helsinki. This *ad hoc* force was composed in the main of Ju 87 dive-bombers and ground-attack Fw 190s. Its fighter element was provided by Hauptmann Rudorffer's II./JG 54.

For the next month the Kuhlmey units were in the air almost without pause in support of the embattled Finns. Targets included enemy troop and tank concentrations, bridges along their lines of supply, and landing craft along both the Gulf of Finland and Lake Ladoga shores of the isthmus. II. *Gruppe's* Focke-Wulfs were hard pressed to cover this sustained level of activity, and lost at least seven pilots to all causes in the attempt. But it was all to no avail. The Soviets succeeded in occupying almost the entire Karelian Isthmus, including the ancient Finnish city of Viipuri (Vyborg) at its northern end, and the *Gefechtsverband* Kuhlmey was disbanded during the latter half of July.

Throughout this time the aerial defence of the Baltic states had rested squarely on the shoulders of just 13(!) Fw 190s of 2. and 3./JG 54. This was all the strength at Hauptmann Ademeit's disposal after his 1. *Staffel* had also been detached to Finland. From 19 June to 15 July 1./JG 54 was stationed at Turku at the entrance to the Gulf of Bothnia to protect German naval vessels operating in that area.

The return of 1. *Staffel* and II. *Gruppe* from their respective expeditions to Finland – the last time the 'Green Hearts' would operate from Finnish soil – had been brought about by the situation along the eastern borders of the Baltic states. The long-threatened storm had finally broken. But even a reunited JG 54, mustering less than 50 serviceable Focke-Wulfs between them, could do little to hinder this latest offensive by the Red army, whose obvious aim was the recapture of the Soviet Union's three Baltic 'provinces'.

By the end of July 18. *Armee* had been pushed back from the Narva positions north of Lake Peipus and 16. *Armee* had relinquished its hold on Pleskau to the south. On the far right-hand flank, Dünaburg (Daugavpils), in southern Latvia, fell on 28 July. JG 54 put up a fierce resistance. The *Geschwader* was responsible for the majority of the 504 enemy aircraft – nearly half of them Il-2s – reported destroyed by *Luftflotte* 1 throughout the month.

By comparison its own losses were relatively low (albeit comprising some 25 per cent of its available strength). In July and August the

Geschwader suffered 11 pilots killed or missing and just one wounded. These figures do, however, include two Knight's Cross holders.

On 7 August Hauptmann Horst Ademeit's aircraft was hit by small-arms fire near Dünaburg, and he went down behind enemy lines. I. *Gruppe's Kommandeur* had a score of 166 at the time of his disappearance. Three weeks later, on 28 August, Oberfeldwebel Wilhelm Philipp of 3./JG 54 was wounded in a clash with Airacobras. After his recovery, Philipp would be transferred to III. *Gruppe* in the west.

Despite their own paucity of numbers, JG 54's pilots continued to inflict severe casualties on the Red Air Force – 15 August saw 2. *Staffel* claim its 1000th victory of the war. It was during August that the two *Gruppen* (and IV./JG 54 currently re-equipping in Poland) began their convoluted transition to the new four-*Staffel* establishment being introduced throughout the *Jagdwaffe*. The process was not fully completed until October, and is again most simply illustrated by the following table:

I./JG 54	1. *Staffel* - as before
	2. *Staffel* - new
	3. *Staffel* - as before
	4. *Staffel* - ex-3./KG 2
II./JG 54	5. *Staffel* - as before
	6. *Staffel* - new
	7. *Staffel* - ex-4. *Staffel*
	8. *Staffel* - ex-4./KG 2
(IV./JG 54	13. *Staffel* - ex-10. *Staffel*
	14. *Staffel* - ex-11. *Staffel*
	15. *Staffel* - ex-12. *Staffel*
	16. *Staffel* - ex-6. *Staffel*)

The lengthy period of reorganisation was not allowed to impede the tempo of operations, but throughout it all, the Red Army continued its remorseless drive westwards. By the end of August the Soviets had advanced beyond Riga and were now only some 75 miles (120 km) from the Baltic coast above East Prussia. 16. and 18. *Armeen* were in danger of

Having served as *Staffelführer* of 5./JG 54 at Immola, Leutnant Heinz Wernicke returned from Finland to take over 1. *Staffel*. On 30 September he was awarded the Knight's Cross for 112 victories. Note that since the abortive attempt on the Führer's life on 20 July, all members of the armed services had been ordered to adopt the *'Deutschen Gruß'* (literally 'German greeting', more commonly the 'Heil Hitler') in place of their normal military salutes as an outward demonstration of loyalty!

Oberfeldwebel Helmut Missner was one of the many experienced frontline pilots of JG 54 who served tours as instructors with the various *Ergänzungsgruppen* in the Reich and occupied territories. Missner was awarded a posthumous Knight's Cross after losing his life while on attachment to 1./ErgGr Ost at Sagan

being trapped in the 'bulge' of Estonia, but during September and early October both armies managed to squeeze through the bottleneck between German-held Riga and the right-hand flank of the Red tide surging past only some 18 miles (30 km) to the south of the city.

To help protect the ground troops' passage *Stab* and I. *Gruppe*, the latter commanded since the loss of Horst Ademeit by Hauptmann Franz Eisenach, transferred from Jakobstadt to Riga-Skulte in the very neck of the gap.

I./JG 54's new *Kommandeur* had previously served as *Kapitän* of 3. *Staffel* before being seriously wounded in December 1943, when his score was standing at 49. Although having been back on operations for only a few weeks, Franz Eisenach had already nearly doubled that total. Nine victories over the Riga area on 14 September took him to exactly 100. Another September 'centurion' was Leutnant Gerhard Thyben, who had joined II. *Gruppe* from JG 3 back in April with 37 kills already to his credit.

Thyben's 100th on 30 September coincided with the award of the Knight's Cross to 1. *Staffel's* long-serving Leutnant Heinz Wernicke for his 112 victories. By now *Stab*, I. and II. *Gruppen* were all occupying Riga-Spilve, a large combined airfield and seaplane base on the opposite (eastern) side of the Latvian capital from the smaller Skulte. It was here that Oberstleutnant Anton Mader relinquished command of the *Geschwader*.

The officer who arrived on 1 October to become JG 54's fifth and final *Kommodore* was Dietrich Hrabak, who had been a fellow *Staffelkapitän* of Mader's in the pre-war I./JG 76, the unit's first reported casualty – brought down behind Polish lines on 3 September 1939, but safely returned twenty-four hours later – and *Kommandeur* of II./JG 54 from August 1940 until October 1942. Having served since then as *Kommodore* of JG 52 on the southern sector, Dietrich Hrabak returned to the 'Green Hearts' with the rank of Oberst and wearing the Oak Leaves.

Early in October two posthumous Knight's Crosses were awarded to members of the *Geschwader* recently lost on operations. 4. *Staffel's* Leutnant Helmut Grollmus was one of those killed in action during II./JG 54's deployment to Finland as part of the *Gefechtsverband* Kuhlmey. With a final score of 75, he had been brought down by ground fire east of Viipuri on 19 June.

Four days after the announcement of Grollmus' award on 6 October, another went to Oberfeldwebel Helmut Missner. It was Missner who had been credited with JG 54's 5000th victory back in July 1943. Latterly, he had been serving as an instructor with EJG 1 in Germany. Since the disbandment of its own *Ergänzungsgruppe* many of JG 54's more experienced pilots had been rotated back to the Reich's training centres for temporary tours of duty to impart their frontline skills and knowledge to youngsters fresh out of flight school.

As the air war over Germany itself intensified, these instructors had begun to be drawn into Defence of the Reich operations. During this little-recorded part of JG 54's history a number of victories were claimed. But, inevitably, casualties had been suffered too, and Helmut Missner was one of them. He was killed on 12 September when he dived into the ground near Sagan from a reported altitude of 21,500 ft (6500 m) due, it is believed, to a failure in his oxygen system.

Meanwhile, in the east, Oberst Hrabak's two *Gruppen* continued to hack away at the Red Air Force. On 10 October Hauptmann Franz Eisenach had received the Knight's Cross for 107 kills. And five days later 6. *Staffel's* Oberleutnant Helmut Wettstein downed the *Geschwader's* 9000th enemy aircraft of the war.

But as so often in the past, individual successes in the air could do little to influence events on the ground, which, as far as JG 54 was concerned, were rapidly approaching their climax. On 9 October Soviet Forces had reached the Baltic Sea near Memel. Forty-eight hours later Riga fell. Shortly before, *Stab* and I. *Gruppe* had withdrawn to Tuckum, some 37 miles (60 km) to the west of the Latvian capital, and II. *Gruppe* had moved to Libau-Grobin on the coast above Memel.

With the Red Army having retaken Lithuania to the south of them, and now standing at the gates of East Prussia, the *Geschwader* – together with their old brothers-in-arms, the 16. and 18. *Armeen* – found itself on the Courland peninsula, cut off from all land contact with the main body of the German forces.

Courland was to be the stage for the last act in the drama of JG 54's wartime career. The stubby peninsula was bounded to the east by the Gulf of Riga and to the west by the Baltic. The Soviets were firmly established along its southern edge, and had occupied the island of Ösel 15 miles (25 km) off its northern tip (separated by the Irben Straits, the scene of Walter Nowotny's three-day dinghy ordeal in 1941).

At first there had been the possibility of a break-out, but Adolf Hitler forbade any such move. On 21 October he ordered all troops on the peninsula to go over to the defensive. The Führer had plans for their later use in a counter-offensive against the right-hand flank of the Red Army's drive into Germany. Nothing ever came of this scheme. As their troops pushed westwards towards the ultimate prize, Berlin, it was the Soviets who mounted an offensive to eradicate the annoying thorn of Courland at their backs.

In fact, no fewer than six separate major offensives would be launched against the Courland pocket during the closing months of the war. But all were repulsed with bloody losses, and the peninsula held out until the very end.

By early November JG 54's 60+ serviceable Fw 190s were deployed about the western half of the Latvian peninsula, with *Stab* and I. *Gruppe* at Schrunden (Skrunda) and Windau (Ventspils), and II. *Gruppe* still at

The fourth member of the 'Nowotny *Schwarm*', Leutnant Rudolf Rademacher, also subsequently served with ErgGr Ost at Sagan. Here, on 30 September, he is presented with his Knight's Cross (for 95 kills) by a familiar figure – the *Inspizient Ost*, ex-*Kommodore* Hannes Trautloft. Rademacher's stick is a memento of wounds received during an attack on US heavy bombers 12 days earlier. Fully recovered, 'Rudi' Rademacher would end the war as a leading Me 262 jet *Experte* (see *Osprey Aircraft of the Aces 17 - German Jet Aces of World War 2* for further details)

The two Knight's Cross winners of 6 December, Leutnants Ulrich Wöhnert and Gerd Thyben, are seen on the Courland front in the winter of 1944-45. They are from the left, Hauptmann Herbert Findeisen (*Kommandeur* of II./JG 54 from February 1945), Wöhnert (5. *Staffel*), Thyben (7. *Staffel*) and Leutnant Hermann Schleinhege (8. *Staffel*, Knight's Cross 19 February 1945)

Libau (Liepaja). Targets were plentiful as the Soviets staged the first of their offensives. On 27 October the *Geschwader* had downed no fewer than 57 enemy machines. The following day Hauptmann Rudorffer was alone credited with a further 11, which took him beyond the double century to a total of 202.

On 1 November 3. *Staffel's* Feldwebel Ulrich Wernitz was awarded the Knight's Cross for his 82nd victory, a Pe-2 destroyed back on 28 August, before a serious illness had rendered him unfit for operations.

A welcome break from the incessant Soviet offensives against the Courland Peninsula as 'Father Christmas', aka Feldwebel Fritz Hangebrauk, visits 7. *Staffel* at Libau-Nord

'Pipifax' Wernitz had often flown as wingman to Otto Kittel, and it was the latter's Swords, announced on 25 November for a score standing close to 230, which highlighted the month. Less than a fortnight later, on 6 December, Knight's Crosses were presented to Leutnants Ulrich Wöhnert and Gerhard Thyben for 86 and 116 kills respectively.

As the above decorations indicate, personal scores kept growing – but the Soviets kept coming. On 14 December two waves of bombers carried out a heavy attack on the town and port facilities of Libau. JG 54's fighters downed 44 of them. But the following day the raiders were back. Although they lost even more on this occasion – the 'Green Hearts' claimed 56 – they caused considerable damage. Eleven aircraft were destroyed on the ground and personnel casualties were high.

On 21 December some 2000 aircraft of the Red Air Force supported Soviet ground forces in launching another major attempt to overrun Army Group North's two battered *Armeen*. Just like the first two onslaughts, however, this latest offensive would also founder on the rock of stubborn German resistance. On the opening day of the 'Third Battle of Courland' the *Geschwader* shot down 42 enemy machines. 3. *Staffel's* highly-experienced Feldwebel Hans-Joachim Kroschinski claimed five Pe-2s in short order, but return fire from the rear gunner of his last victim – his 76th in total – severely wounded Kroschinski. On 17 April 1945 'Kroschi' Kroschinski, whose terrible injuries had cost him his eyesight and one of his legs, would be honoured with the Knight's Cross.

Also among December's casualties was Leutnant Heinz Wernicke, the *Kapitän* of 1. *Staffel*, who was killed in a mid-air collision with his wingman, Unteroffizier Wollien, on 27 December. Forty-eight hours later 8. *Staffel's* Unteroffizier Karl Hagel was reported missing after attacking a formation of Il-2s. His was the last loss of the year, and the only one sustained by the two Courland *Gruppen* on 29 December – in stark contrast to III./JG 54's experiences over the Reich on that date.

Among I. and II./JG 54's more important tasks towards the end was the protection of the ungainly and vulnerable minesweeping Ju 52s – nicknamed *Mausis* – as they sought to keep open the vital sea lanes supplying beleaguered Courland

But it was over the fighting front that the 'Green Hearts' suffered their greatest loss when Oberleutnant Otto Kittel was shot down in action against Il-2s on 14 February 1945. Pictured here early in his career, the 'Quiet NCO' gives little indication that he will become the fourth most successful fighter pilot in the entire Luftwaffe

Against a background of Libau-Nord's concrete bunkers, the 'Indestructible 6th' set off on a sleigh ride. On the docile panje pony is Feldwebel Anton 'Toni' Meissner, and at the reins is *Staffelkapitän* Hauptmann Helmut Wettstein

It was later calculated that by the end of December 1944, JG 54 had destroyed 9141 enemy aircraft since hostilities had commenced. This made the 'Green Hearts' the second most successful *Jagdgeschwader* of the entire Luftwaffe. Only the redoubtable JG 52 in the southern sector had claimed more.

The new year on the Courland front saw no ambitious *Bodenplatte*-type gesture, just a grim determination to continue resistance in the face of near-constant Soviet pressure. In the last 18 weeks of their war in the east, JG 54's two *Gruppen* would be credited with a further 300+ victories. They would also suffer a handful of casualties each month – and they would be rewarded with a final round of decorations.

On 25 January Major Erich Rudorffer was awarded the Swords for 210 kills. It was on this day that Army Group North, which a week earlier had been ordered by Hitler to give up five of its divisions to help shore up the central sector, was renamed Army Group 'Courland' (*Heeresgruppe 'Kurland'*). On 3 February, having successfully repulsed the Soviets' fourth major offensive, the depleted 16. and 18. *Armeen* were divested of yet more divisions.

By now JG 54 was also having to husband its resources – especially fuel. All supplies had to be brought in by sea and, to a lesser extent, by air, and restrictions were beginning to be placed upon the *Geschwader's* operations. It was only allowed to intervene over the front if ground forces were under direct enemy threat. But pilots continued to patrol the vital sea lanes into Libau and Windau, protecting the small convoys, and even single ships, against attack by Soviet aircraft and torpedo-boats. These supply lines were also heavily mined by the Russians, and another of JG 54's tasks was to fly cover for the vulnerable minesweeping Ju 52s of *Minensuchgruppe* 1 (MSGr 1) as they strove to keep open the maritime corridor to the western Baltic.

But it was over the frontline that the 'Green Hearts' suffered their most grievous loss of 1945. During the second week of February the Red Air Force launched a massive assault on German positions around Dzukste, south of Tuckum, in preparation for the opening of the Soviet's fifth major offensive. JG 54 did what it could to protect the units of 16. *Armee* holding that part of the line. Shortly after midday on 14 February a *Schwarm* of 2./JG 54's Fw 190s, led by *Staffelkapitän* Oberleutnant Otto Kittel, left Zabeln and set course south-east for the 32-mile (50km) flight to Dzukste. Oberfähnrich Renner was one of the three *Schwarm* members;

'At an altitude of 150 m (500 ft), we engaged a formation of 14 Il-2s flying in line-astern attacking ground targets. The *Schwarm* broke into the line of Il-2s from the side. Positioned 100 m (330 ft) off Oberleutnant Kittel's right wing, I saw him attack an Il-2 from behind and below while to our rear another two Il-2s climbed steeply away. A moment later there were flashes around his (Kittel's) cockpit and the machine banked to the right, going down in a shallow glide. The aircraft hit the ground

right wing first and immediately burst into flames. It slid about 200 m (660 ft) to the edge of a nearby wood where it burned out completely. I observed no parachute.'

It was presumed that Kittel had been hit by fire from one of the Il-2s' rear-gunners. Since joining JG 54 in the autumn of 1941 Otto Kittel had destroyed at least 267 Soviet aircraft. He was the *Geschwader's* highest scorer. And with his death, as one of his 2. *Staffel* comrades confessed, 'for us darkness fell in the Courland pocket'.

Generaloberst Kurt Pflugbeil, GOC *Luftflotte* 1 – 'Papa' to his men, but not to his face – congratulates 8./JG 54's Leutnant Hugo Broch on his Knight's Cross. On the left is Broch's *Staffelkapitän* Leutnant Hermann Schleinhege, and this shot was taken at Cirava, Courland, on 12 March 1945

Despite their isolated position, the pilots of JG 54 kept their sense of humour – albeit sometimes of the gallows kind – right up until the last. Oberfähnrich Schreiber has not been strung up for defeatism (a not uncommon occurrence on other fronts during the final weeks of the war), rather he is merely acting the fool under the gas alarm next to one of Libau-Nord's bunkers. Fortunately, this marvel of technology – a short length of railway track and a hammer for hitting it – was never sounded

But the struggle went on. On 19 February 8./JG 54's Leutnant Hermann Schleinhege received the Knight's Cross for some 90 victories. Five days later fellow *Staffelkapitän* Oberleutnant Gerhard Thyben of 7./JG 54 claimed four kills to take his total to 150. II. *Gruppe* had some time earlier made the short hop from Libau-Grobin to Libau-Nord. Although much smaller – it was situated on a tiny square of open ground between the two entry canals to Libau's naval port and commercial harbour – the latter field did have one distinct advantage. The large concrete bunkers along its edge, dating back to the navy's occupation of the area in World War 1, offered perfect protection against the increasingly frequent Soviet air attacks.

It was at Libau-Nord during February that Major Erich Rudorffer took leave of II. *Gruppe* to assume command of the Me 262-equipped II./JG 7 back in the Reich. His replacement for the final few weeks of the war was Knight's Cross-wearing Hauptmann Herbert Findeisen, who had scored 42 kills during his previous service as a tactical reconnaissance pilot.

As the end neared, the *Geschwader*, still with a considerable strength of 70+ serviceable Fw 190s, maintained its ties to its comrades on the ground, with Oberst Hrabak's *Stab* and II. *Gruppe* being based at Cirava and Libau in the western half of the peninsula – territory held by 18. *Armee* – and I. *Gruppe* continuing to occupy Zabeln in the eastern sector defended by 16. *Armee*.

JG 54 may have been abundantly equipped with aircraft, but it lacked the fuel to fly them. When operations were carried out, they were invariably flown in just *Schwarm* or *Rotte* strength. Although few in number, the *Geschwader's* abilities still engendered a healthy respect in their opponents, as this unsolicited testimonial from a Soviet fighter pilot captured at the time illustrates;

'The fighters with the green heart are usually in the minority in any dogfight. But when they are around things always get hot. They are all aces!'

The last two 'aces' to be decorated were 8. *Staffel's* Leutnant Hugo Broch, who was awarded the Knight's Cross on 12 March for 79 victories, and Oberleutnant Gerhard Thyben, *Kapitän* of 7. *Staffel*, whose recent 150 won him the Oak Leaves on 8 April.

Exactly one month later it was all over. The order for the capitulation of all German armed forces, signed by *Großadmiral* Karl Dönitz on 7 May (Adolf Hitler had committed suicide in his Berlin bunker one week earlier),

contained a special addendum referring specifically to *Heeresgruppe* Kurland. It read, in part, '. . . the utmost effort must be made to implement every possibility of evacuation by sea'.

The 'Green Hearts', however, had ways of looking after their own. All non-essential ground personnel had long ago been sent back to the two *Gruppen's* support bases at Neuhausen and Heiligenbeil, in East Prussia. Now, while the Fw 190s were topped up with the last remaining drops of fuel for the long flight westwards across the Baltic and surrender to British forces in Schleswig-Holstein and Denmark, the radios were being removed from the fighters' rear fuselage bays. And as each pilot took off, he carried with him his chief mechanic crammed into the narrow space behind him.

Among the last to leave, on the morning of 8 May, were Oberleutnant Gerhard Thyben and his wingman Feldwebel Friedrich Hangebrauk. Adjusting to the unaccustomed weight at their backs, the pair set out across open sea. As the smoke from burning Libau slipped away over the horizon astern, Gerhard Thyben spotted a lone reconnaissance Pe-2 flying north across their path, and obviously intent on searching the sea lanes for signs of evacuation shipping. Instinct took over. It was the work of seconds to dive out of the rising sun and, in two quick passes, send the enemy machine into the sparkling waters of the Baltic.

Oberleutnant Thyben's victim was one of the last casualties of the air war in Europe. It was certainly the last of JG 54's nearly 9500 victories since Leutnant Gutezeit's 'P.24' had gone down near Warsaw on the opening day of the conflict. The cost to the 'Green Hearts' and their predecessors had been almost 650 pilots killed or missing.

Leutnants Schleinhege and Thyben leave II./JG 54's ops building after a briefing at Libau-Nord in the early months of 1945. A lot has happened in the nearly seven years since the men and machines of Austria's *JaGeschw* II joined the German Luftwaffe in the spring of 1938. But one thing has remained constant throughout – the *Gruppe* badge. Although no longer carried on the unit's Focke-Wulfs, there, on the sign above the door, is the 'Lion of Aspern' . . .

. . . and, by a strange twist of fate, the other *Gruppe* badge dating back to the days of the Polish campaign was still in evidence too. Hauptmann Hellmut Wettstein, the *Staffelkapitän* of 6./JG 54, arrives in Denmark after a long flight across the Baltic Sea to surrender to the British. Behind him is Unteroffizier Asche and, right, one of their two rear-fuselage passengers. Like all members of the *Wehrmacht* who fought on the Courland Peninsula, Wettstein was entitled to wear the campaign cuff title on his left sleeve. This silver-grey band bore the word 'Kurland', which was flanked on the side by an elk's head, and on the other – just visible here – by the 'Crusaders' Cross'

APPENDICES

APPENDIX 1

COMMANDING OFFICERS

Kommodores of the *Jagdgeschwader 'Grünherz'*

Mettig, *Maj* Martin	1/2/40	to	24/8/40
Trautloft, *Obstlt* Hannes	25/8/40	to	6/7/43
von Bonin, *Maj* Hubertus	6/7/43	to	15/2/43 (+)
Mader, *Obstlt* Anton	28/1/44	to	30/9/44
Hrabak, *Oberst* Dietrich	1/10/44	to	8/5/45

Gruppenkommandeure
I./JG 54 (Ex-I./JG 70)

Kithil, *Maj*	7/39	to	15/9/39
von Cramon-Taubadel, *Maj* Hans-Jürgen	15/9/39	to	27/12/39
von Bonin, *Hptm* Hubertus	28/12/39	to	1/7/41
von Selle, *Hptm* Erich	2/7/41	to	20/12/41
Eckerle, *Hptm* Franz	20/12/41	to	14/2/42 (+)
Philipp, *Hptm* Hans	17/2/42	to	1/4/43
Seiler, *Maj* Reinhard	15/4/43	to	6/7/43
Homuth, *Maj* Gerhard	1/8/43	to	3/8/43 (+)
Götz, *Olt* Hans (acting)	3/8/43	to	4/8/43 (+)
Nowotny, *Hptm* Walter	21/8/43	to	4/2/44
Ademeit, *Hptm* Horst	4/2/44	to	8/8/44 (+)
Eisenach, *Hptm* Franz	9/8/44	to	8/5/45

II./JG 54 (Ex-I./JG 76)

von Müller-Rienzburg, *Hptm* Wilfried	1/4/38	to	9/1/40
Blumensaat, *Maj* Albert	10/1/40	to	5/2/40
Kraut, *Maj* Richard	5/2/40	to	10/7/40
Winterer, *Hptm*	11/7/40	to	14/8/40
Hrabak, *Hptm* Dietrich	26/8/40	to	27/10/42
Hahn, *Hptm* Hans	19/11/42	to	21/2/43
Jung, *Hptm* Heinrich	21/2/43	to	30/7/43 (+)
Rudorffer, *Hptm* Erich	1/8/43	to	2/45
Findeisen, *Hptm* Herbert	2/45	to	8/5/45

III./JG 54 (Ex-I./JG 21)

Mettig, *Maj* Martin	15/7/39	to	2/2/40
Ultsch, *Hptm* Fritz	3/2/40	to	5/9/40 (+)
Scholz, *Olt* Günther (acting)	6/9/40	to	4/11/40
Lignitz, *Hptm* Arnold	4/11/40	to	30/9/41 (+)
Seiler, *Hptm* Reinhard	1/10/41	to	15/4/43
Schnell, *Hptm* Siegfried	5/43	to	11/2/44
Patzak, *Olt* Rudolf (acting)	2/44	to	21/2/44
Klemm, *Hptm* Rudolf (acting)	2/44	to	3/44
Sinner, *Hptm* Rudolf	3/44	to	10/3/44
Schroer, *Hptm* Werner	14/3/44	to	20/7/44
Weiss, *Hptm* Robert	21/7/44	to	29/12/44 (+)
Dortenmann, *Olt* Hans (acting)	1/45	to	1/45
Heilmann, *Olt* Wilhelm (acting)	1/45	to	14/2/45
Klemm, *Maj* Rudolf	14/2/45	to	25/2/45

III./JG 54 (second formation)

Schlosstein, *Hptm* Fritz-Karl	3/45	to	4/45

IV./JG 54

Rudorffer, *Hptm* Erich	7/43	to	30/7/43
Sinner, *Hptm* Rudolf	8/43	to	11/2/44
Schnell, *Hptm* Siegfried	11/2/44	to	25/2/44 (+)
Koall, *Hptm* Gerhard (acting)	2/44	to	5/44
Späte, *Hptm* Wolfgang	5/44	to	30/9/44
Klemm, *Hptm* Rudolf	1/10/44	to	12/2/45

Kapitän/Kommandeure ErgSt – ErgGr/JG 54

Zilken, *Olt*	10/40	to	3/41
Eggers, *Olt*	3/41	to	3/42

(+) – Killed or Missing In Action

APPENDIX 2

AWARD WINNERS

All JG 54 winners of the Knight's Cross, and its higher grades, are presented here chronologically, with their scores at the time of the award(s) noted in brackets

	Knight's Cross		Oak Leaves		Swords		K/MIA
Hrabak, *Hptm* Dietrich	21/10/40	(16)					
Philipp, *Olt/Hptm* Hans	22/10/40	(20)	24/8/41	(62)	12/3/42	(82)	
Lignitz, *Olt* Arnold	5/11/40	(19)					(+)
Bob, *Olt* Hans-Ekkehard	7/3/41	(19)					
Trautloft, *Maj* Hannes	27/7/41	(20)					
Mütherich, *Olt* Hubert	6/8/41	(31)					(+)
Pöhs, *Lt* Josef	6/8/41	(28)					
Ostermann, *Lt/Olt* Max-Hellmuth	4/9/41	(29)	10/3/42	(62)	17/5/42	(100)	(+)
Eckerle, *Hptm* Franz	18/9/41	(30)	12/3/42	(59)*			(+)
Späte, *Olt* Wolfgang	5/10/41	(45)	23/4/42	(72)			
Seiler, *Hptm* Reinhard	20/12/41	(42)	2/3/44	(100)			
Kempf, *Ofw* Karl	4/2/42	(41)					
Beisswenger, *Lt* Hans	9/5/42	(47)	30/9/42	(100)			(+)
Hannig, *Lt* Horst	9/5/42	(48)					
Stotz, *Ofw* Max	16/6/42	(53)	30/10/42	(100)			(+)
Wandel, *Hptm* Joachim	21/8/42	(64)					(+)
Nowotny, *Lt/Hptm* Walter (1)	4/9/42	(56)	4/9/43	(189)	22/9/43	(218)	
Sattig, *Hptm* Karl	19/9/42	(53)*					(+)
Schilling, *Ofw* Wilhelm	10/10/42	(46)					
Siegler, *Fw* Peter	3/11/42	(48)*					(+)
Heyer, *Lt* Hans-Joachim	25/11/42	(53)*					(+)
Götz, *Olt* Hans	23/12/42	(48)					(+)
Zweigart, *Ofw* Eugen-Ludwig	22/1/43	(54)					(+)
Rupp, *Lt* Friedrich	24/1/43	(50)					(+)
Broennle, *Ofw* Herbert	14/3/43	(57)					
Fink, *Olt* Günther	14/3/43	(46)					(+)
Ademeit, *Lt/Hptm* Horst	16/4/43	(53)	2/3/44	(c.120)			(+)
Kittel, *Ofw/Olt* Otto	29/10/43	(123)	14/4/44	(152)	25/11/44	(c.230)	(+)
Jung, *Hptm* Heinrich	12/11/43	(68)*					(+)
Lang, *Lt/Olt* Emil	22/11/43	(119)	11/4/44	(144)			
Wolf, *Ofw/Olt* Albin	22/11/43	(117)	27/4/44	(144)*			(+)
Scheel, *Lt* Günther	5/12/43	(71)*					(+)
Sterr, *Ofw* Heinrich	5/12/43	(86)					(+)
Loos, *Lt* Gerhard	5/2/44	(85)					(+)
Döbele, *Lt* Anton	26/3/44	(94)*					(+)
Philipp, *Ofw* Wilhelm	26/3/44	(61)					
Weiss, *Olt/Hptm* Robert	26/3/44	(70)	12/3/45	(121)*			(+)
Tegtmeier, *Ofw* Fritz	28/3/44	(99)					
Rudorffer, *Maj* Erich (2)			11/4/44	(130)	25/1/45	(210)	
Teumer, *Olt* Alfred	19/8/44	(76)					
Brandt, *Ofw* Paul	29/9/44	(30)					(+)
Wernicke, *Lt* Heinz	30/9/44	(112)					(+)
Grollmus, *Lt* Helmut	6/10/44	(75)					(+)

	Knight's Cross	Oak Leaves	Swords	K/MIA
Eisenach, *Hptm* Franz	10/10/44 (107)			
Missner, *Ofw* Helmut	10/10/44 (82)*			(+)
Wernitz, *Fw* Ulrich	1/11/44 (82)			
Klemm, *Hptm* Rudolf	18/11/44 (40)			
Thyben, *Lt* Gerhard	6/12/44 (116)	8/4/45 (c.150)		
Wöhnert, *Lt* Ulrich	6/12/44 (86)			
Hoffmann, *Lt* Reinhold	28/1/45 (66)*			(+)
Schleinhege, *Lt* Hermann	19/2/45 (c.90)			
Broch, *Lt* Hugo	12/3/45 (79)			
Kroschinski, *Lt* Hans-Joachim	17/4/45 (76)			

(+) – Killed or Missing In Action during service with JG 54

* – Awarded posthumously

(c.) – Circa

(1) – Hptm Walter Nowotny was the only member of JG 54 to receive the Diamonds, awarded 19/10/43 for 250 kills

(2) – Lt Erich Rudorffer received the Knight's Cross as a member of JG 2, awarded 1/5/41 for 19 kills

APPENDIX 3

SCORES

Unit Scores

	Number of Victories	Areas
Stab JG 54	165	East
I./JG 54	3564	mainly East
II./JG 54	3621	mainly East
III./JG 54	1500	mainly West
IV./JG 54	550	East, West, Reich
Erg/JG 54	51	East
Total	**9451**	

Individual Scores

Number of JG 54 pilots with 200+ victories:	4
Number of JG 54 pilots with 100+ victories:	20
Number of JG 54 pilots with 50+ victories:	58
Number of JG 54 pilots with 20+ victories:	114

APPENDIX 4

REPRESENTATIVE ORDERS OF BATTLE

1/1/39
Poland

				Est/Serv
I./JG 21	*Hptm* Mettig	Gutenfeld	Bf 109D	46 - 46
I./JG 76	*Hptm* Müller-Rienzburg	Ottmütz	Bf 109E	51 - 45
				Totals: 97 - 91

10/5/40
France

Stab JG 54	*Maj* Mettig	Böblingen	Bf 109E	4 - 4
I./JG 54	*Hptm* von Bonin	Böblingen	Bf 109E	42 - 27
I./JG 21	*Hptm* Ultsch	München-Gladbach	Bf 109E	46 - 34
I./JG 76	*Obstlt* Kraut	Ober-Olm	Bf 109E	46 - 39
				Totals: 138 - 104

13/8/40
Battle of Britain   Est/Serv
Stab JG 54	*Maj* Mettig	Campagne-les-Guines	Bf 109E	4 - 2
I./JG 54	*Hptm* von Bonin	Campagne-les-Guines	Bf 109E	34 - 24
II./JG 54	*Hptm* Winterer	Hermelinghen	Bf 109E	36 - 32
III./JG 54	*Hptm* Ultsch	Guines-South	Bf 109E	42 - 40

Totals: 116 - 98

5/4/41
Balkans
Stab JG 54	*Maj* Trautloft	Graz-Thalerhof	Bf 109E	3 - 3
II./JG 54	*Hptm* Hrabak	Graz-Thalerhof/Arad	Bf 109E	32 - 24
III./JG 54	*Hptm* Lignitz	Arad	Bf 109E	42 - 39

Totals: 77 - 66

21/6/41
Russia (*Barbarossa*)
Stab JG 54	*Maj* Trautloft	Lindental	Bf 109F	4 - 3
I./JG 54	*Hptm* von Bonin	Rautenberg	Bf 109F	40 - 34
II./JG 54	*Hptm* Hrabak	Trakehnen	Bf 109F	40 - 33
III./JG 54	*Hptm* Lignitz	Blumenfeld	Bf 109F	40 - 35

Totals: 124 - 105

20/7/42
Russia (Leningrad)
Stab JG 54	*Maj* Trautloft	Siverskaya	Bf 109F	4 - 3
I./JG 54	*Hptm* Philipp	Krasnogvardeisk	Bf 109F/G	43 - 27
II./JG 54	*Hptm* Hrabak	Ryelbitzi	Bf 109F/G	40 - 28
III./JG 54	*Hptm* Seiler	Siverskaya	Bf 109F	27 - 21

Totals: 114 - 79

31/8/43
Russia (post-*Zitadelle*)
Stab JG 54	*Maj* von Bonin	Siverskaya	Fw 190A	2 - 2
I./JG 54	*Hptm* Nowotny	Poltava	Fw 190A	23 - 15
II./JG 54	*Hptm* Rudorffer	Kiev	Fw 190A	29 - 14
IV./JG 54	*Hptm* Sinner	Siverskaya	Bf 109G	33 - 19

Totals: 87 - 50

26/7/44
Normandy
III./JG 54	*Hptm* Weiss	Villacoublay	Fw 190A	30 - 16

1/1/45
Reich (*Bodenplatte*)
III./JG 54	*Olt* Dortenmann (acting)	Fürstenau	Fw 190D-9	20 - 17
IV./JG 54	*Hptm* Klemm	Vörden	Fw 190A	43 - 25

Totals: 63 - 42

1/4/45
Courland
Stab JG 54	*Obstlt* Hrabak	Cirava	Fw 190A	5 - 4
I./JG 54	*Hptm* Eisenach	Zabeln	Fw 190A	35 - 32
II./JG 54	*Hptm* Findeisen	Libau-Nord	Fw 190A	44 - 41

Totals: 84 - 77

COLOUR PLATES

1

Fiat CR.32bis '179' of I./JG 138, Wien-Aspern, Summer 1938

I./JG 138's ex-Austrian Air Force Fiat CR.32bis biplanes initially remained in their silver finish, only the national markings being repainted to indicate the change of ownership (*see photos*). During the later spring/early summer of 1938 at least some of the 20+ Fiats on strength were given a coat of what appears to have been standard Luftwaffe 70/71 camouflage. It was also at this time that the *Gruppe* badge first appeared. This was the coat-of-arms of Aspern, a part of Greater Vienna since 1905, but just a small village a century earlier when it was the site of decisive defeat for Napoleon's armies.

2

Avia B 534 'Yellow 14' of I./JG 70, Herzogenaurach, Summer 1939

I./JG 70's flirtation with the even more esoteric Avia B 534 was equally brief. Only one *Staffel* was equipped with the Czech machines, 3./JG 70 being formed from the Avia *Lehrgang* (training course) currently resident at Herzogenaurach at the time of the *Gruppe's* activation there. Unlike the Fiats of I./JG 138, the Avias did not need to be camouflaged. They were left in their ex-Czech Air Force standard dark olive, and even retained the Avia company trademark on the tailfin. Only the national insignia required amendment, with *Balkenkreuze* being added to fuselage and wings, and the Swastika replacing the Czech roundel on the rudder. Although a Luftwaffe-style numeral has been added, there is no sign yet of the *Gruppe* badge.

3

Bf 109D-1 'Yellow 10' of I./JG 21, Arys-Rostken, September 1939

Formed from a cadre of personnel supplied by I./JG 1, the new I./JG 21 also took over the former's complement of Bf 109Ds (I./JG 1 was then in the process of re-equipping with *Emils*). While keeping the previous owner's *Staffel*-identifying spinner decorations, I./JG 21 altered the *Gruppe* badge slightly by changing the background of the Crusaders' Cross from white to red. It then added a touch of its own by introducing individual *Staffel* badges. 'Yellow 10' wears 3./JG 21's relatively short-lived 'swooping falcon' device.

4

Bf 109E-1 'White 2' of I./JG 76, Stubendorf, September 1939

A change of designation and a change of equipment for the Vienna *Gruppe*, but the badge is still in evidence (and would remain so for four more years). Bearing textbook finish and markings of the early war years, Wk-Nr. 3349 was among the first *Emils* to be taken on charge by I./JG 76. It was reportedly flown on occasion by *Staffelkapitän* Oberleutnant Dietrich Hrabak after his return to the unit following the forced-landing of his own 'White 1' (Wk-Nr. 3311) behind Polish lines on 3 September 1939.

5

Bf 109E-1 'Red 9' of I./JG 21, Le Mans, Summer 1940

Early in 1940 the Bf 109's 'official' role changed from one of metropolitan defence to that of air superiority. This was reflected in the new camouflage scheme, introduced prior to the *Blitzkrieg* in the west, which saw the *hellblau* (light grey-blue) of the undersurfaces carried upwards to include the fuselage sides and vertical tail surfaces. Points of interest here are the retention of the 2. *Staffel* spinner decoration (as originally worn by I./JG 1), the *Staffel* badge, the larger size fuselage *Balkenkreuz* (although still of the pre-war narrow-bordered variety) and the individual aircraft numeral now placed ahead of the cockpit.

6

Bf 109E-1 'White 11' of III./JG 54, Guines-South, August 1940

When I./JG 21 was redesignated III./JG 54 in the period between the Battles of France and Britain, the *Gruppe's* elaborate spinner markings began to disappear. The late summer of 1940 was a time of transition as far as markings and camouflage were concerned, and many anomalies occurred. The plain *hellblau* flanks of 'White 11' have already been toned down by overspraying. This, together with the yellow cowling and rudder, date it as well into the Battle of Britain. Yet this early *Emil* has been repainted with a pre-war style and size fuselage cross – and combines it with a regulation 1940 Swastika positioned on the tailfin.

7

Bf 109E-3 'White Double Chevron' of Hauptmann Hubertus von Bonin, *Gruppenkommandeur* I./JG 54, Campagne-les-Guines, September 1940

This somewhat drab machine, the mount of I./JG 54's *Kommandeur*, is much more heavily-dappled than 'White 11' above, and lacks any kind of yellow tactical markings. Note the 'hollow'-style command insignia. This method of displaying the chevrons in outline only (in either black or white) was uncommon, but not unique. Still no sign of a *Gruppe* badge, though. The cartoon below the cockpit was originally the emblem of 3. J/88, the *'Mickymaus' Staffel* of the *Legion Condor*, with whom von Bonin had scored four kills in Spain.

8

Bf 109E-4 'White 1' of Oberleutnant Hans Philipp, *Staffelkapitän* 4./JG 54, Campagne-les-Guines, October 1940

Looking much more the 'archetypal Battle of Britain '109', Hans Philipp's 'White 1' displays the obligatory Wien-Aspern *Gruppe* badge and a rudder scoreboard marking the start of a career which would put him among the 12 most successful pilots of the entire Luftwaffe. The last three of the 18 kill bars illustrated here represent a trio of No 66 Sqn Spitfires claimed on 13 October (the RAF squadron did suffer three aircraft crashed or forced-landed on that date, but two were subsequently repaired). Two more claims would win 'Fips' Philipp the Knight's Cross nine days later.

9

Bf 109E-4 'Black Double Chevron' of Hauptmann Dietrich Hrabak, *Gruppenkommandeur* I./JG 54, Graz-Thalerhof, April 1941

This machine wears the distinctive 'crazy-paving' three-tone camouflage finish applied to II. *Gruppe's Emils* early in 1941. The yellow cowling and aft fuselage band are Balkan theatre markings. According to the regulations the rudder should have been yellow, too, but has escaped repainting presumably to preserve Hrabak's scoreboard showing his 16 kills to date. After the successful conclusion of the campaign in Yugoslavia, II./JG 54 converted to Bf 109Fs, which were finished in a similar camouflage scheme to that shown. Hrabak's mount continued to soldier on at a fighter training school in France, still wearing the markings depicted here!

10

Bf 109F-2 'Yellow 1' of Oberleutnant Hans Schmoller-Haldy, *Staffelkapitän* 4./JG 54, Sarudinye, August 1941

Wearing a more common, nondescript mottle overall, this early *Friedrich*, pictured in the opening months of the campaign in the east, is noteworthy for its individual markings. Not only does it sport 3. *Staffel's* 'Huntsman' badge on the cowling, it also carries a miniature *'Mickymaus'* (see profile 7) ahead of the fuselage numeral. Hans Schmoller-Haldy was another ex-member of the *Legion Condor's* 3. J/88, but arriving towards the close of the civil war, he did not achieve any victories in Spain.

11

Bf 109E-7 'White 12' of 1.(Eins)/JG 54, Windau, September 1941

Representative of the *Emils* flown by the trainee pilots of the *Einsatzstaffel* over the Baltic shortly after the launch of *Barbarossa*, this E-7 wears a white spinner and large white numerals (from its previous service in France) combined with yellow eastern front theatre markings. It has not been possible to ascertain whether the 'Viking ship' unit badge is that of the *Einsatzstaffel* alone, or of the entire *Eragänzungsgruppe* (nor have the colours shown been fully confirmed). This same badge was later applied to some of the *Friedrichs* operated by 1.(Eins)/JG 54 from Siverskaya during the winter of 1941-42.

12

Bf 109F-2 'Black 8' of III./JG 54, Siverskaya, November 1941

Also based at Siverskaya during the first winter of the eastern front campaign, many of III. *Gruppe's* F-2s were given a very rudimentary coat of white winter camouflage, which was applied to just the wing and tailplane upper surfaces and along the dorsal spine. 8. *Staffel's* 'Piepmatz' (cheeky sparrow) badge has survived the transition from 2./JG 21 (see profile 5). And note that the mid-1940 redesignation has finally resulted in the addition of a III. *Gruppe* wavy bar. Two further points: since arriving in Russia the *Staffel's* red numerals have given way to black to avoid confusion with the predominantly red markings of Soviet Air Force machines. And the soon-to-be-famous 'Green Heart' is beginning to make its appearance on the *Geschwader's* fighters.

13

Bf 109F-2 'Black Chevron and Bars' of Hauptmann Hans Philipp, *Gruppenkommandeur* I./JG 54, Krasnogvardeisk, March 1942

Recently transferred from nearby Siverskaya, Hans Philipp's F-2 (wearing the fuselage insignia of a *Major beim Stab*) has had the benefit of a more thorough winter camouflage point job, and has also had its mainwheel leg covers removed the better to cope with the snow and icy conditions. Since his 16 kills of mid-October 1940 (see profile 8), 'Fips' Philipp is now rapidly approaching his century (achieved on 31 March 1942). Note, for the first time, the Nürnberg coat-of-arms badge of I. *Gruppe* and, again, the 'Green Heart' emblem.

14

Bf 109F-2 'Black 8' of Feldwebel Otto Kittel, I./JG 54, Krasnogvardeisk, May 1942

By the spring of 1942 I. *Gruppe's* badge and the *Geschwader* emblem were both firmly established. Here they are seen on the dark green splinter-camouflaged *Friedrich* of one Otto Kittel, an unassuming NCO pilot of 2. *Staffel*, whose 15 kills to date – which had taken almost a year to achieve – gave no indication of his future rise to prominence as the highest-scoring 'Green Heart' of all. With a final total of 267 Soviet aircraft destroyed at the time of his own loss in February 1945, the then Oberleutnant Kittel ranks as the fourth most successful fighter pilot in aviation history.

15

Bf 109F-4 'White Double Chevron' of Hauptmann Reinhard Seiler, *Gruppenkommandeur* III./JG 54, Siverskaya, Summer 1942

After being appointed *Kommandeur* of III. *Gruppe* late in 1941, 'Seppl' Seiler seems to have dispensed with the personal 'Top Hat' emblem which had adorned most of his previous machines (*see photo page 43*). This was another reference to prior service with the *Legion Condor*. The 'Top Hat' had been the badge of 2. /J88, with whom Seiler had claimed nine Republican kills between August 1937 and February 1938. Another apparent casualty is the meticulous rudder scoreboard which had been a regular feature of Seiler's previous mounts, and which is conspicuously absent here. Could this be the CO's reserve aircraft, or is that perhaps a replacement rudder?

16

Bf 109F-2 'White 8' of Leutnant Walter Nowotny, 1./JG 54, Ryelbitzi, Summer 1942

Very similar markings and finish to profile 14 (and also, coincidentally, bearing the individual numeral '8'), this splinter-camouflaged *Friedrich* is distinguished by the 'lucky 13' superimposed on the 'Green Heart', and by the rudder scoreboard displaying 43 kill bars. It is the aircraft flown by Walter Nowotny, undoubtedly the most charismatic of all the many *Experten* to serve with JG 54. With his tally seen here only 13 short of the 56 which would win him the Knight's Cross on 4 September 1942, 'Nowi's' career was just about to take off!

17

Bf 109G-2 'White Chevron and Bars' of Major Hannes Trautloft, *Geschwaderkommodore* JG 54, Siverskaya, Summer 1942

Vying with Walter Nowotny as arguably the most famous 'Green Heart' of them all, Hannes Trautloft – the man who introduced the *Geschwader's* striking motif – could not compete with his Austrian subordinate in terms of numbers of enemy aircraft destroyed. Hannes Trautloft's final tally of 45 Soviet kills was modest by eastern front standards. His great strength lay in his natural qualities of leadership and his care for those under his command. All of the *Kommodore's* later machines, like the *Gustav* depicted here, featured the badges of his three component *Gruppen* superimposed in miniature on his own *Geschwader* emblem.

18

Bf 109G-2/R6 'Yellow 7' of II./JG 54, Zhitomir, February 1943

The second Russian winter saw elements of JG 54 being despatched to other sectors of the eastern front. This cannon-armed 'Gunboat' of 6. *Staffel* was used in action against Soviet air and ground targets in the Ukraine early in 1943. Its badly weathered appearance reflects the severity of the conditions, and the growing demands made upon the *Jagdwaffe* as Soviet pressure increased all along the front. It was in an aircraft of this type that II. *Gruppe's Kommandeur*, Major Hans 'Assi' Hahn, was lost when he was forced to land behind enemy lines on 21 February 1943.

19

Fw 190A-4 'Black Chevron and Bars' of Oberstleutnant Hannes Trautloft, *Geschwaderkommodore* JG 54, Krasnogvardeisk, February 1943

While II. *Gruppe's Gustavs* were battling it out along the central and southern sectors, *Stab* and I./JG 54 had been converting onto the Fw 190, the machine they would fly until the end of the war. The command insignia and three small *Gruppe* badges incorporated into the 'Green Heart' emblem on this particular example reveal it to be the aircraft of the now Oberstleutnant Hannes Trautloft – although the fresh patch of paint ahead of the fuselage *Balkenkreuz* suggests it may have already had one previous owner.

20

Fw 190A-4 'White 9' of Feldwebel Karl Schnörrer, I./JG 54, Krasnogvardeisk, February 1943

Numbered among 1./JG 54's first batch of Focke-Wulfs, 'White 9' is already showing signs of wear and tear on its carefully applied coat of overall winter white. This was the machine normally allocated to 'Quax' Schnörrer, who regularly flew as wingman to his *Staffelkapitän*, Leutnant Walter Nowotny, at this stage of the war.

21

Fw 190A-4 'White 10' of Leutnant Walter Nowotny, *Staffelkapitän* 1./JG 54, Krasnogvardeisk, Spring 1943

In all probability originally camouflaged white overall as Schnörrer's aircraft immediately above, Nowotny's 'White 10' now reveals large segments of its basic dark green finish – the washable white distemper being easily removed – in order to blend it in more effectively with the Russian landscape during the period of the spring thaw.

22

Fw 190A-4 'White 2' of Oberfeldwebel Anton Döbele, I./JG 54, Krasnogvardeisk, Spring 1943

'Toni' Döbele's Fw 190 has presumably been subject to the same treatment as Nowotny's (above) to make it less conspicuous against the patchy terrain during the last of Russia's spring thaw. Döbele was the third member of the celebrated 'Nowotny *Schwarm*', whose amazing run of

success between March and November 1943 made it justly famous throughout the eastern theatre.

23

Fw 190A-5 'Black 5' of Oberleutnant Max Stotz, II./JG 54, Siverskaya, late Spring 1943

After its deployment to the Ukraine and other points south earlier in the year, II. *Gruppe* had also begun to re-equip with Fw 190s – conversion was complete by the late spring/early summer of 1943. 'Black 5' wears one of the two known camouflage schemes sported by the unit's new Focke-Wulfs at this period – a combination of spray-blended two dark greens over all uppersurfaces. It also wears a standard set of eastern front theatre markings, and both *Gruppe* and *Geschwader* badges . . . but the latters' days were already numbered.

24

Bf 109G-4/R6 'Black 6' of III./JG 54, Oldenburg, May 1943

By the spring of 1943 III. *Gruppe* was fighting a very different kind of war. Transferred to the west but deemed unsuitable for Channel front operations, its pilots found themselves in northern Germany helping to defend the homeland against attack from US heavy bombers. Their standard grey 'Gunboats' were initially devoid of all unit and personal markings, with the only splash of colour being provided by the yellow undersides to the machines' engine cowlings.

25

Fw 190A-5 'Black 7' of Leutnant Emil Lang, II./JG 54, Siverskaya, May 1943

A new sense of anonymity was also beginning to impinge upon the eastern front. An official edict sought to ban all unit badges in an attempt to deny intelligence to the enemy as to aircraft dispositions and movements. Many *Geschwader* seem to have ignored these instructions, but not so JG 54. The patch of fresh green paint on the cowling of 5. *Staffel's* 'Black 7' marks the demise of the 'Lion of Aspern', which had identified all II. *Gruppe* machines since the days of the Fiat biplanes. I./JG 54's short-lived Nürnberg shield had already fallen victim – note the tell-tale darker patch on Döbele's 'White 2' (profile 22).

26

Fw 190A-5 'Black 12' of Fähnrich Norbert Hannig, 5./JG 54, Siverskaya, circa May 1943

Although Hannes Trautloft's famous 'Green Heart' emblem lasted a little longer (more importance was placed on the removal of *Gruppe* badges to disguise the movements of a *Geschwader's* individual components), this too was soon to disappear. When new aircraft, such as 'Black 12' seen here in a pristine northern sector summer finish of light brown and greens, began arriving in the late spring of 1943, they no longer bore any trace of the proud unit heraldry which had been such an integral part of JG 54's fighters over the preceding months and years.

27

Fw 190A-6 'White 12' of Leutnant Helmut Wettstein, *Staffelkapitän* 1./JG 54, Shatalovka-East, September 1943

An early example of the new order – complete anonymity cloaks this two-tone green summer camouflaged A-6. Or does it? Although also sometimes seen on JG 51 aircraft,

JG 54's invariable practice of centring the aft fuselage yellow theatre band level with, and as a background to, the *Balkenkreuz* provides a hefty clue as to unit ownership. 'White 12' was flown by Leutnant Helmut Wettstein, Nowotny's successor as *Kapitän* of 1. *Staffel*.

28

Fw 190A-6 'Black Double Chevron' of Hauptmann Walter Nowotny, *Gruppenkommandeur* I./JG 54, Vitebsk, November 1943

Appointed *Kommandeur* of I. *Gruppe* in August 1943, Walter Nowotny has observed the ban on unit badges, but allows himself two individual touches. His personal 'lucky 13', which used to adorn the *Geschwader's* 'Green Heart' on his earlier *Friedrichs* (see profile 16), has now reappeared beneath the cockpit sill. Smaller still, the miniature '8' tucked between the inner arms of the command chevrons is believed to be a reference to his once-favoured individual aircraft numeral.

29

Bf 109G-6 'Yellow 1' of Oberleutnant Wilhelm Schilling, *Staffelkapitän* 9./JG 54, Ludwigslust, February 1944

Somewhat ironically, it was now the 'detached' III. *Gruppe* in the west which would keep the 'Green Heart' flying (or beating?). Here the *Geschwader* emblem is worn as a background to III./JG 54's original 'Crusaders' Cross' shield of I./JG 21 vintage. Both are slightly smaller than in earlier presentations, as is the 'Grinning devil' badge of 9. *Staffel* on the cowling. Now an integral part of the Defence of the Reich organisation, III. *Gruppe's* machines also sport the blue fuselage band allocated to JG 54.

30

Fw 190A-8 'Black 5' of III./JG 54, Villacoublay, June 1944

Re-equipped with Focke-Wulfs immediately prior to D-Day, III. *Gruppe's* machines were rushed to France still in their full Defence of the Reich finery. This Fw 190's markings are thus very similar to those of the *Gustav* immediately above, albeit with the individual aircraft letter and III. *Gruppe* vertical bar in black to indicate 8. *Staffel*. Note, however, that there is no longer any sign of a *Staffel* badge, and that at some stage since first arriving in the west (see profile 24) III./JG 54 has changed its long-standing wavy bar *Gruppe* symbol to the now more common vertical style depicted here and on Schilling's G-6.

31

Fw 190A-6 'Black Double Chevron' of Hauptmann Erich Rudorffer, *Gruppenkommandeur* II./JG 54, Immola, June 1944

Back to the less flamboyant markings of the eastern front, this somewhat drab mottled grey machine with lighter cowling and tailfin was the mount of Erich Rudorffer, JG 54's third-highest scorer (after Kittel and Nowotny). Pictured at the time of the unit's brief deployment to Finland in mid-1944, the fighter features a white-black spiralled spinner and retains (although much reduced in size) II. *Gruppe's* 'open ended' style of command chevron.

32

Fw 190A-8 'White 3' of Oberleutnant Karl Brill, *Staffelkapitän* 10./JG 54, Lublin, July 1944

Another unit to uphold the 'Green Heart' tradition was IV.

Gruppe. Activated on *Gustavs* in East Prussia in mid-1943 to make up for the recent 'loss' of III./JG 54 to the west, the *Gruppe* began converting to the Fw 190 a year later. At the same time a new unit badge was introduced. This latter featured a stylised version of the coat-of-arms of Königsberg, the capital of East Prussia, reproduced in miniature on a green heart – it is seen here on the cowling of Brill's 'White 3'. Note also the 'Indian's head' emblem of 10. (later 13.) *Staffel*, and the truncated 'wavy bar' marking, a device used by many IV. *Gruppen* during the later stages of the war.

33

Fw 190A-6 'White Chevron and Bars' of Oberstleutnant Anton Mader, *Geschwaderkommodore* JG 54, Dorpat, Estonia, July 1944

One of the machines flown by JG 54's penultimate *Kommodore* was this A-6, wearing a segmented camouflage of faded brown and green – a not uncommon finish during the summer months on the northern sector of the front, and one particularly favoured by tactical reconnaissance units. It is estimated that Anton Mader claimed some 18 Soviet aircraft destroyed during his eight-month tenure of office.

34

Fw 190A-6 'Yellow 5' of Oberleutnant Otto Kittel, I./JG 54, Riga-Skulte, September 1944

Since his early days as an 'unknown' with 2. *Staffel* (see profile 14), Otto Kittel had been transformed. It was the conversion from Bf 109s to Fw 190s which triggered his remarkable rise. Having been credited with 150 victories back in April 1944, Kittel, now flying with 3./JG 54, was about to achieve his double century as the *Geschwader* withdrew to the Courland Peninsula (although there is nothing to indicate the fact on this very plain 'Yellow 5'). Returning to 2./JG 54 as *Staffelkapitän*, Kittel's score had climbed to 267 by the time he was killed in action on 14 February 1945.

35

Fw 190A-8 'White 1' of Leutnant Heinz Wernicke, *Staffelkäpitan* 1./JG 54, Riga-Spilve, September 1944

Like Otto Kittel, Heinz 'Piepl' Wernicke was another long-serving ex-NCO member of I. *Gruppe* since commissioned and risen to the position of *Staffelkapitän*. He too would lose his life over the Courland pocket, killed in a mid-air collision (with his wingman) during a dogfight on 27 December 1944. Again, this drably anonymous A-8, wearing the simplified markings of the closing months of the war, offers no indication that its pilot was a 100+ *Experte*.

36

Fw 190A-8 'Black 6' of IV./JG 54, Mörtitz, November 1944

Having twice been all but annihilated – first on the central sector of the eastern front during the summer of 1944, and again when sent to oppose the Allied airborne landings around Arnhem in September – IV./JG 54 finally took its place in the Defence of the Reich organisation in the late autumn of 1944. As such, the unit's Focke-Wulfs, like those of III. *Gruppe* (profile 30), also wore the blue fuselage band allotted to JG 54, although the two *Gruppen* never operated together. It is clear from 14. *Staffel's* 'Black 6'

125

depicted here that unit badges (as shown in profile 32) were no longer carried.

37

Fw 190A-8 'Black Double Chevron' of Hauptmann Franz Eisenach, *Gruppenkommandeur* I./JG 54, Schrunden, November 1944
During the last six months on the Courland Peninsula the aircraft of I. and II. *Gruppen* were of a drab uniformity. Only the command insignia or individual numeral distinguished one from the other. The simple black double chevron on this A-8 identifies it as the machine flown by Franz Eisenach, an ex-*Zerstörer* pilot who commanded I./JG 54 for the last nine months of the war.

38

Fw 190A-8 'White 12' of Oberleutnant Josef Heinzeller, *Staffelkapitän* 1./JG 54, Schrunden, December 1944
Its otherwise overall dapple grey camouflage alleviated only by a black-white spiralled spinner, 'White 12' was the mount of Oberleutnant Josef Heinzeller, who replaced the fallen Heinz Wernicke at the head of 1. *Staffel* late in December. Heinzeller survived the war with 35 victories to his credit.

39

Fw 190D-9 'Black 4' of III./JG 54, Varrelbusch, December 1944
In September 1944 III./JG 54 had been selected as the first *Gruppe* to convert to Kurt Tank's latest design, the Fw 190D-9, popularly known as the 'Long Nose'. This example, 'Black 4' of 10. *Staffel*, is representative of the finish and markings worn by the unit's machines towards the close of the year. As far as is known, the 'Long Noses' did not carry JG 54's blue Defence of the Reich bands around their rear fuselages, but several sported personal emblems and names. The machine illustrated may have been the 'Black 4' lost on 29 December 1944, III./JG 54's 'Blackest day', while being flown by 11. *Staffel's* Unteroffizier Werner Rupp.

40

Fw 190A-9 'Yellow 1' of Hauptmann Helmut Wettstein, *Staffelkapitän* 6./JG 54, Libau-Nord, February 1945
Having earlier succeeded Walter Nowotny as *Staffelkapitän* of 1./JG 54 (see profile 27), and then scored the *Geschwader's* 9000th victory in October 1944, Helmut Wettstein ended the war at the head of 6. *Staffel*. His bulged-canopy A-9 offers one last glimpse of a typical eastern front 'Green Heart' fighter as hostilities neared

their close – no badges, no theatre markings, just a purposeful fighting machine of the sort which would continue to oppose the Soviet Air Force right up until the very last day.

41

Fw 190A-8 'Black 12' of III./JG 54, Eggersdorf, March 1945
By contrast, the final throes of 'JG 54' in the west (more accurately, in the Reich) had very little at all to do with the 'Green Hearts'. In late February 1945 a second III. Gruppe was created from a *Zerstörer* unit (II./ZG 76). Consisting of only three *Staffeln* (9., 10. and 11.), its operational history was brief in the extreme. This machine of 10. *Staffel* is typical of the aircraft flown by the unit – simplified national insignia and a flattened 'wavy bar' more akin to a late-war IV. *Gruppe* symbol than to a III. The diagonal white stripe across the face of the tail swastika was a feature of several of these III./JG 54 aircraft, although whether it served as a tactical marking or a 'political statement' is not known.

42

Fi 156C 'SB+UG' of I./JG 54, Krasnogvardeisk, February 1943
Like all *Jagdgeschwader*, JG 54 was provided with outside transport aircraft (Ju 52s, Me 323s and the like) when a major redeployment or transfer took place. But each of the 'Green Heart' *Gruppen* also had their own light communications machines for general day-to-day requirements. This winter-camouflaged, ski-equipped Storch leaves no room for doubt as to its rightful owners. The *Geschwader* emblem and I. *Gruppe* badge say it all.

43

Go 145A 'PV+HA' of II./JG 54, Sarudinye, August 1941
One of II. *Gruppe's* resident 'hacks' during the early days of the campaign in the east was this two-seat Gotha trainer. Although fully camouflaged, and complete with yellow theatre markings – a mirror image of II./JG 54's *Friedrichs*, in fact – the 'Lion of Aspern' can hardly ever have graced a less warlike machine.

44

Kl 35D 'BD+QK' of III./JG 54, Siverskaya, August 1942
Not to be outdone, the pilots of III./JG 54 had this smart little runabout for their daily chores. Or perhaps, if that proprietary 'Winged clog' motif on the engine cowling of this beautifully camouflaged and maintained Klemm is anything to go by, it was reserved for the sole use of 7. *Staffel*.

SELECTED BIBLIOGRAPHY

CONSTABLE, TREVOR J and TOLIVER, COL RAYMOND F, *Horrido! Fighter Aces of the Luftwaffe.* Macmillan, New York, 1968

DIERICH, WOLFGANG, *Die Verbände der Luftwaffe 1935-1945.* Motorbuch Verlag, Stuttgart, 1976

FRAPPE, JEAN BERNARD, *La Luftwaffe face au Débarquement Alliée.* Editions Heimdal, Bayeux, 1999

GABRIEL, ERICH (ed), *Fliegen 90/71: Militärluftfahrt und Luftabwehr in Österreich von 1890 bis 1971.* Heeresgeschichtliches Museum, Vienna, 1971

GROEHLER, OLAF, *Kampf um die Luftherrschaft.* Militärverlag der DDR, Berlin 1988

HARDESTY, VON, *Red Phoenix, The Rise of Soviet Air Power, 1941-1945.* Arms and Armour Press, London, 1982

HAUPT, WERNER, *Kurland 1944/1945, Die vergessene Heeresgruppe.* Podzun-Pallas-Verlag, Friedberg, 1979

HEILMANN, WILLI, *Alert in the West: A German Fighter Pilot's Story.* William Kimber, London, 1955

HELD, WERNER, *Die deutschen Jagdgeschwader im Russlandfeldzug.* Podzun-Pallas-Verlag, Friedberg, 1986

HELD, WERNER, TRAUTLOFT, HANNES and BOB, EKKEHARD, *Die Grünherzjäger: Bildchronik des Jagdgeschwaders 54.* Podzun-Pallas-Verlag, Friedberg, 1985

KÖHLER, KARL, et al, *Abwehrkämpfe am Nordflügel der Ostfront 1944-1945.* Deutsche Verlags-Anstalt, Stuttgart, 1963

KUROWSKI, FRANZ, *Balkenkreuz und Roter Stern, Der Luftkrieg über Russland.* Podzun-Pallas-Verlag, Friedberg, 1984

MEHNERT, KURT und TEUBER, REINHARD, *Die deutsche Luftwaffe 1939-1945.* Militär-Verlag Patzwall, Norderstedt, 1996

MEISTER, JÜRG, *Der Seekrieg in den osteuropäischen Gewässern 1941/45.* J F Lehmanns Verlag, Munich, 1958

NOWARRA, HEINZ J, *Luftwaffen-Einsatz 'Barbarossa' 1941.* Podzun-Pallas-Verlag, Friedberg

OBERMAIER, ERNST, *Die Ritterkreuzträger der Luftwaffe 1939-1945: Band 1, Jagdflieger.* Verlag Dieter Hoffmann, Mainz, 1966

PARKER, DANNY S, *To Win the Winter Sky: Air War over the Ardennes 1944-1945.* Greenhill Books, London, 1994

PLOCHER, GENERALLEUTNANT HERMANN, *The German Air Force versus Russia, 1942.* Arno Press, New York, 1966

PLOCHER, GENERALLEUTNANT HERMANN, *The German Air Force versus Russia, 1943.* Arno Press, New York, 1967

PRICE, DR ALFRED, The Luftwaffe Data Book. Greenhill Books, London, 1997

PRIEN, JOCHEN, et al, *Die Jagdfliegerverbände der Deutschen Luftwaffe 1943 bis 1945, Teil 1: Vorkriegszeit und Einsatz über Polen - 1934 bis 1939.* Struve's Buchdruckerei und Verlag, Eutin, 2000

PRIEN, JOCHEN and RODEIKE, PETER, *Messerschmitt Bf 109F, G and K Series.* Schiffer, Atglen, 1993

RAMSEY, WINSTON G (ed), *The Battle of Britain Then and Now.* After the Battle, London, 1985

RODEIKE, PETER, *Focke-Wulf Jagdflugzeug: Fw 190A, Fw 190 'Dora', Ta 152H.* Rodeike, Eutin, 1999

SCHRAMM, PERCY ERNST (ed), *Kriegstagebuch des OKW (8 Vols).* Manfred Pawlak, Herrsching, 1982

SCUTTS, JERRY, *Jagdgeschwader 54 Grünherz: Aces of the Eastern Front.* Airlife, Shrewsbury, 1992

SHORES, CHRISTOPHER, et al, *Fledgling Eagles.* Grub Street, London, 1991

URBANKE, AXEL, et al, *Mit Fw 190D-9 im Einsatz.* VDM Heinz Nickel, Zweibrücken, 1998

VÖLKER, KARL-HEINZ, *Die deutsche Luftwaffe 1933-1939.* Deutsche Verlags-Anstalt, Stuttgart, 1967

ZIEMKE, EARL F, *Stalingrad to Berlin: The German Defeat in the East.* Center of Military History, Washington DC, 1968

INDEX

References to illustrations are shown in **bold**. Colour plates are shown with page and caption locators in (brackets).